SELF PUBLISHING IN CANADA

A complete guide to designing, printing and selling your book

Other books by Suzanne Anderson:

Good Morning Quadra: The History of the HMCS Quadra

SELF PUBLISHING IN CANADA

A complete guide to designing, printing and selling your book

Suzanne Anderson

Half Acre Publishing
Duncan, British Columbia

Canadian Cataloguing in Publication Data

Anderson, Suzanne 1953 -
   Self-Publishing in Canada: a complete guide to designing, printing and selling your book/ Suzanne Anderson. — 1st ed.

Includes bibliographical references and index.
ISBN 1-894208-00-5

   1. Self-publishing—Canada. I. Title.

   Z285.5.A54 2003   070.5'93'0971
   C2003-905581-7

Half Acre Publishing
7311 Bell McKinnon Road
Duncan, British Columbia V9L 6A8

Printed in Canada

Dedication

To my husband, Bob, whose love and support proves that he is a true modern day literary patron.

TABLE OF CONTENTS

ACKNOWLEDGEMENTS

Although writing is a solitary activity, a book cannot be written without support from family, friends, and professional colleagues. I wish to sincerely thank everyone who has given me their encouragement, and have worked to make this project a reality.

Bob Anderson, Gary Backlund, Janice Beaveridge, Janice Beecher, Chris Behm, Virginia Brucker, Dawn Butler, Malcolm Butler, Robyn Filiatrault, Miro Francisty, Paul Grey, Jan Harcus, Eliza Hemingway, Dawn Hoebee, Daniel Hurley, Lisa Kearns, Gerry Patenaude, Tom Paterson, Dan Poynter, Pat Robinson, Karen Watson, and Oscar Zemlak.

FOREWORD

*I don't want people to die with a book still
inside them.*
— Dan Poynter

When I started self-publishing 34 years ago,
I had to learn the hard way – by trial and error.
Since then I have made it my personal quest to
make sure that anyone who wants to publish
their own book learns how to do it right. I have
written several books on the subject and lecture
worldwide.

I believe in self-publishing as the best way to
get your book out to the public. You will make more
money, which everyone wants, get to press sooner
and have complete control of your book. This is
more important than you realize. You should be the
one who picks out the book's title and decides
where to sell your book. After all, bookstores are
not necessarily the places to sell books. Who will
know your market better than you?

While Canada and the United States have
much in common, there are enough differences in

resources and business practices to merit this book. I believe Canada needs a book like this. Right now more and more people are starting to self-publish. With the information gathered from this, and other books, you will acquire the knowledge to do it professionally and successfully.

– Dan Poynter
The Self Publishing Manual
Author-publisher who has coached thousands of successful publishers

PREFACE

Self-publishing is no longer the last resort for rejected writers – it has become a viable choice in the publishing game. With today's technology and the internet, anyone can do it. As the trade publishing houses cope with financial and marketing problems, there is a large niche opening up for those of us who want to do it ourselves. We are people who want control of our books and know the best way to market them. The problem for most writers is that they do not know how to publish their own book.

Because I did not know what steps to take the first time I self-published, I checked out every book on the subject from my local public library (which is something I recommend). I ended up purchasing many of them for my personal library. I discovered that there are many good books on self-publishing and marketing, but most of them were written in the United States. While about 60% of the content of these books gives information that is useful across the border, the remainder are specific to the U.S.

It was apparent that we needed a comprehensive guide to self-publishing in Canada. We need to know about GST/HST, business startup information for all the provinces, and especially Canadian resource lists. We need to understand how differently copyright, ISBN, and CIP data are handled on our side of the border. Quite plainly, self-publishing and marketing are very different between the two countries. As more writers turn to self-publishing, I hope this book will help fill that gap.

CHAPTER ONE
The Writer's Dream

Listen and learn and find your dream.
When you have found it, don't give up.
— Alwyn Morris
Champion Canoeist

THE DREAM

Most writers dream of the day when they will see their book in print. The scene unfolds with a letter from a publisher offering to purchase your manuscript. You work with a professional editor who helps you turn the manuscript into the best writing you could imagine doing. An array of people design the pages and covers, and a whole department is available to market your book. All you have to do is revise and rewrite if necessary. When all these people get finished with your manuscript, it is a book! It becomes your success story and sells in bookstores. This dream keeps many new writers going.

The reality is that you send queries to publisher after publisher. You receive letters thanking you, BUT your book is not right for their list for one reason or another. This is assuming you even receive a reply. You might have a book for an audience you are familiar with and write great letters pitching ideas for promotion, but there simply are not enough publishers to print all the manuscripts in Canada. It is estimated that only 1 in 10 manuscripts will get into print. The dream begins to sound like a nightmare. But do not despair. There is a way to become published.

WHY SELF-PUBLISH

If you are reading this book, the events I describe are probably familiar to you. You, like many others, have decided that if no one is willing to publish your book then you will do it yourself. You will take the chance and, if it arrives, the money and fame.

Many well known authors and books come from the self-publishing field. Mark Twain, A.A. Milne, Lord Byron, Edgar Allen Poe, and Beatrix Potter were self-published. More recently *The Celestine Prophecy, The Christmas Box,* and *Bridges of Madison County* started out as self published books which were picked up by a trade publisher and went on to become international bestsellers. *The Wealthy Barber, Company's Coming* cookbooks and *The Looney Spoons Cookbook* are Canadian self-published books that have become best sellers. Unfortunately there is a stigma to self-publishing. It has been felt for too long that people publish their own books because they are not good enough for a "real" publisher to handle it. Self publishing has been long thought of as the place of last resort used by rejected writers. Well they are wrong! In the next decade, more and more of our reading material will come from author-publishers. As computer technology improves, and the trade publishers become even more dollar driven, a whole new niche is opening up for people who are willing to do it themselves. Self-publishing is quickly becoming a chosen option.

Self-publishing is both demanding and gratifying. You have control of the whole program. You design the cover, choose the price, and decide where and when the book will be distributed. You start your own publishing company and can take advantage of tax deductions. Of course you have already been doing this as a writer, haven't you? The really neat thing about self-publishing is that you get to keep all the money you make on the book.

The standard royalty contract with an established publishing company gives a first time writer 7-10% on the book (or retail) price. Sometimes you can get a bit higher percentage if it is paid on the wholesale price. Unless you are already famous, the advance will barely cover the expenses you incurred researching and writing your book. Then you only receive a royalty cheque once or twice a year. With self-publishing you start making money with the first book you sell. Except for production expenses, the money is all yours.

One of the major advantages to self publishing is the amount of time it takes to turn your manuscript into a book. It is possible to have your books ready to sell in less than eight weeks. A traditional publisher could take as long as one or two years to make this happen. The sooner your books are available for sale, the sooner you start making money.

When you self publish, you retain all the rights to your book. Many potential authors do not realize the trade publisher will own the rights to their book. Since they put out the funds to have it published, this is part of their pay off. It is fair, but many find it frustrating that a book they spent months or years on, will not even legally belong to them. All they have is the copyright. This leads us to the fact that self publishers also have full control over their work. A person who self publishes make all the decisions concerning editing, content, cover, title, and marketing. Often new authors are shocked to find out they have no control over what their book will look like or be titled.

Self-publishing sounds all too easy. And maybe it is. It is also time consuming, costs money, and has its own language. Self-publishing is quite simple. At the same time it is complex. What this book hopes to do is explain the whole process to you. I recommend you first read this book from cover to cover. Only then will you know what you are up against. Then you can make an informed decision as to whether you want to go through with self-publishing your book. Never forget this is a business. By doing your homework, you should not end up as one of the hundreds of businesses in this country that fail every year.

TYPES OF PUBLISHERS
Trade Publishers

There are many kinds of publishers. The most well known are the big ones such as McClelland & Stewart Inc, whose stable of authors ranges from Margaret Atwood to Alice Munro. They are the big players in the Canadian publishing industry. They produce the most best sellers and have the biggest publicity budgets. Because of the cost of competition and producing books, they are not able to give new authors as much of a chance as they could many years ago.

There are medium and small publishers who take more chances with the kinds of books that the large publishers cannot afford to do. These usually are poetry books or specialty books that appeal to a smaller, or niche, audience. Small presses allow the writer more input into the production, marketing, and distribution of their book, however, these days even the small publishers are driven by the cost of producing and marketing a book.

In the trade publishing industry, too many books are being produced because the marketing department decides what will sell. A novice author can be disillusioned to discover this. For most of this century, editors have discovered new authors, designers have made a product appealing to the reading public, and the marketing department has sold the books. In the past few years it seems that editors and designers have to make decisions based on what the marketing department thinks will sell well and, not only recover the cost of production, but make a profit.

Bookstores are changing too. In the past few years, the small local bookstores that welcomed regional books are being pushed aside by the large chain stores. Known as "box" stores, they have enormous floor space and usually support a coffee bar or cafe. These types of bookstores are expensive to run because they try to open in prime retail sites. They cannot afford to carry stock that is not selling for very long. Unsold books are returned to the publisher (who already sold it for a discount) for a full refund. Trade publishing is a tough industry.

University Presses

Many Canadian universities operate small publishing houses. They release from six to thirty titles a year. The one exception is University of Toronto Press with 125 to 130 releases a year. They publish non-fiction, and primarily scholarly or trade books. Check under Book Publishers in *The Canadian Writer's Market* for details on what each press is looking for. Perhaps your manuscript will fall into a subject area covered by a university press, and you can have your book published for you. Keep in mind that the university presses are still in the same situation as trade publishers. In other words, they need to make a profit.

Subsidy Publishing

If you want to be published badly enough, and have lots of money, you can pay someone to do it for you. The country is full of subsidy publishers who will produce a book for you. These types of publishers are referred to in the industry as "vanity publishers" because some people will pay anything to see their name in print. Unfortunately, there are many who charge the author too much money and develop an inferior product. Many book reviewers will not even read a book with a subsidy press label on it. Subsidy publishers require a lot of research. Although the first place to find one is under *Publishers* in the Yellow Pages, the next place to go is the Better Business Bureau. Subsidy publishers do not give your manuscript the benefit of good editing. They do not guarantee a good product either. Often the books fall apart easily. If you choose to deal with this type of publisher remember you are paying for a product they have no interest selling. After spending a large sum of money, you still have to market your book yourself.

All that being said, a subsidy publisher might be right for you. It will depend on what you plan to do with your book. If you are putting together a family history or a chapbook of poetry that you do not plan to sell, then this might be your best option. You decide what you want and receive a product to give to family or friends. Whether a review will look at it or not is of no importance. Subsidy publishing does fill a need.

A recent hybrid of the subsidy publisher is the print-on-demand (POD) publisher. For a sum of money they assist you with ordering required information for your legal page, send two books to the National Book Deposit, put your book into their online bookstore, print your book, and give you a "complimentary" five or ten books. If you want more books, you have to pay for them. While the concept of "one book as you need it" is what they promote, they charge a lot less per unit when you buy several books. This is what you would expect from a regular offset printer, which the POD companies claim are more expensive. They also insist you use their publishing name, which means you lose control of your book. As I mentioned earlier, if you only plan on a short run of books to be given away rather than sold, this is a possible solution for you.

Desktop Publishing

A fairly new entry into the publishing arena is the desktop publishing centre. Often these people have years of publishing experience and walk the new author through the process with expert advice along the way. They have in-house resources such as designers and typesetters, and act as a consultant during the process. Most do not print books, but will help you find a printer. They do not help you market your book either. Fees vary, so make sure you check out at least three DTP centres and compare prices to services. Also be sure to have the company show you other books they have helped to publish.

Book Production Companies

Unlike the Desktop Publishing companies, these folks work with the new author until the book is actually in print. Some even help market your book. They charge a flat fee per book. Although there are many reputable companies of this kind, be careful when you deal with them.

Some companies charge the flat rate and then add on extra fees. One new author had her bill increase by 50% by the time she received her books. Make sure you understand the contract. When in doubt, see a lawyer. One visit will not cost you thousands of dollars, but that is what it could save you.

As with subsidy publishers, check to see what imprint or publisher's name will be on the book. If you intend to truly self publish, you have to have your own publishing name in the book. One option would be to share publishing rights. The legal page would say "in cooperation with..." and give both names.

Co-op Publishing

Sometimes several people get together to pool their skills and produce a book or several books. They share the work right up to the printing process. This can save money on editing, design, typesetting, and layout. Then the group shares the cost of marketing. This group form of self-publishing requires less individual financial investment. Before getting involved with co-op publishing, make sure everyone's part is spelled out clearly. More importantly, be clear on the financial obligation of every member of the group. Misunderstandings can cause hard feelings among members of the group, which will defeat the original purpose and affect productivity.

E-Publishing

Online publishing firms purchase manuscripts, pay royalties, and make writers' books available to the public just like a traditional trade publisher. In this case, though, they do not print your book on paper, but make it available on the internet. Customers can either read the beginning of the book and decide if they want to download it, or they can download it immediately. The e-book is purchased online, and that is how authors are able to receive royalties. Since the cost of production and paper is not necessary, there is usually a profit to pay royalties form.

Like any publisher, you have to do your homework and check out the online publishing companies. Some offer a straight deal like you would receive from a regular trade publisher, and others offer to share the financial cost. Check to see what types of computers and readers the firm can download it to. It is important for an e-publishing firm to keep up with the latest technology in order to make your book available to the greatest number of readers. A good e-publisher should have editors who will work with you the same as that of a trade publisher. Check out e-publishers at ***http://ebookconnections.com*** for detail on various Canadian and American publishers.

Self-publishing

A concept that has been around for centuries, self-publishing has been made even easier with the development of computer technology. You can produce a manuscript with word processing software that will give you, among other things, word count, sentence length, font type, and even set up your titles and subtitles. In the newer word processing programs you can completely format your text. This means you can set up such things as page size, font type and size, page numbers, the table of contents, and chapter heads. Some even have the ability to make an index. If you know how to use a desktop publishing program you can format even more professionally. Both of these will take you to the point where you produce a *galley*. As long as the final copy is printed on either a laser or high quality ink jet printer, the galley is ready to go to a book printer. Computers make self-publishing an attainable goal for everyone. If you do not know how to use one, you probably have a friend or family member who does. And for those who view the new technology with real trepidation, you can still hire someone to typeset and format your manuscript.

As an author-publisher you are in control of the whole process from beginning to end. This gives you much greater opportunity to be creative. After all, you wrote the book so you should know best what to call it, what it should look like, and who would want to buy it. Unlike trade published books, you call the shot on everything. For example, you might think you have the perfect title for your book. Trade publishers normally change the title of a book unless you are really insistent, which is not a good idea for a new author. By self-publishing, you do not have to make compromises.

When you self-publish, you decide how to market your book. Should it be marketed by mail order or through a distributor? If you want the latter, do you think it should be a regional distributor or a national one? What is the purchase price of the book going to be? You might be able to hook up with a corporation that will want your book as a product tie-in to either sell or give away. You may be a natural salesperson. If so, you have a chance of being successful selling your books. If you, or someone you know, has computer skills you could build your own website. Most e-mail providers will give you web space. Sometimes it even comes for free with your account.

You can have your books on the shelf much more quickly if you self-publish. It could take a trade publisher anywhere from one to three years to release a book. Publishing yourself could have it in your hands (or basement or garage) in as little as six to eight weeks. This puts it in the bookstore much more quickly and allows you to start making money more quickly, too.

One of the nicest things about self-publishing is that you will get to keep all the profits you make from the book. Since you are going to be in business for yourself, you can take advantage of income tax breaks. Of course many of these tax breaks were available to you as an author (see Revenue Canada's *Tax Information for Professional Artists*), but now you can take advantage of even more tax opportunities.

All this control and money sounds wonderful. Just remember, this is a small business with all the headaches that can come with it. While there are many positive aspects about being self employed, you are still the one who is responsible for all decisions. If you, the novice publisher, make mistakes, then you, the business person, will pay for them. You will not have the services of a professional editor unless you hire one. You will not have the benefit of an experienced publicist unless you hire one. You may not have an artistic bone in your body so designing a cover will be a formidable task. There are not many books available on how to design book covers, so you would have to either take your chances or hire a graphic designer. Designing the interior of the book may be a large job too. Again, you can hire someone to format the book for you or muddle through yourself. Remembering that an amateur looking book will not sell very well, you then have to decide if you want to spend money on professionals or risk losing money on an unpopular product. Either way, it is going to cost you money.

FINANCING

When you self-publish you also have to have the funds to pay up front for the book's production. This amount can vary from hundreds of dollars to thousands of dollars. First you have to find the funding to produce the book. Then you have to spend money and work hard to market the book. Otherwise you will end up with boxes and boxes – and boxes – of books stored in your house or garage. This leads you to doubt your book and your ability to write. But it may not be your writing you should question, just your uninformed decisions.

So where does one find money to become a self-publisher? There are many sources. Some of them might work for you and others definitely will not. The most obvious place to start is with yourself. If you have money in savings, a line of credit, or can take out a second mortgage on your home you can come up with the funds. You might see if you can get a loan from the bank or your credit card, but this will saddle you with payments before you have a chance to sell any books. Another source would be family members who are either willing to loan the money or would become a partner in this venture. It is doubtful if you would find investors unless you plan on going into publishing in a big way. If you receive money from someone other than yourself or your family, go to a lawyer and have a contract drawn up. This could save a lot of grief in the future.

The most well known story of financing a self-published book is about Ottawa sisters Janet and Greta Podleski who co-wrote *Looney Spoons*, a best selling cookbook. They both quit their jobs to work on the project. They used up their savings, maxed out their credit cards, and sold just about everything they owned of value – including Janet's wedding dress. They even had an enormous bake sale to raise money. In their case, the risk paid off handsomely. Not only is their book a bestseller in both Canada and the United States, they have published a second book. They also give nutritional advice on the radio and are being considered for a television show.

There is no easy way to put it – you have to spend money to self-publish. The actual amount will depend on the trim size and page count of your book. The number of books you decide to print will make up your largest cost. Like in any small business, one misstep can be expensive. Before you start self-publishing, you have to learn as much as you can about this particular business. If you have no experience in business at all, you have to learn about that too. If you are not a patient person, and do not want to study either publishing or business, you could lose money.

Self-publishing can be the most gratifying thing you do in your life. The thrill of seeing your book in print and on bookshelves is tremendous. At the same time it could become the biggest and most expensive nightmare of your life. Take your time to learn the business and you will have a good chance at success. You may not make a lot of money, but you will be able to proudly tell others you are an author. This is great for a writer's confidence. When starting out, most of us feel uncomfortable telling people we are writers. They immediately want to know what we have written. Once you publish your book, you will now realize that you are a "real" writer and not just a "wannabe". You can proudly take your place alongside other Canadian authors, whether famous or not. Each one of us contributes to Canada's heritage. And, hey, isn't that worth taking a chance on?

CHAPTER TWO
All That Technical Stuff

For us, fantasy is just reality waiting for a
technology to give it birth.
– Frank Zingrone
Communications Theorist

PICK A SUBJECT

Some topics work better for self-publishing than others. Non-fiction, how-to, and poetry books work especially well. This is not to mean you cannot produce good fiction or a children's illustrated book. But they are tough to market. Right now memoirs, regional histories, and family history stories are hot topics to write about. They lend themselves well to being self-published because they can be done in small print runs if necessary. They are also of interest to a smaller market, where self-publishing is ideal. Many trade publishers, whether large or small, cannot afford to take on a project with a small market. It is just not financially feasible for them.

When you pick your subject, remember you will have to know as much or more about it than anyone who might read your book. In other words, you have to become an expert. Readers have expected you to have done all the research. They expect you to be very knowledgeable about the subject. Do not let them down. The first book I wrote was the history of a Naval training facility known as a "stone ship". I spent three full years researching and writing the book. Unless you are writing a memoir (from memory) you have to learn as much detail about your subject as possible in order to give your reader the full benefit of the material. Skimp on this and people will not want to read your book. Worse, present less than well researched material and you will get lousy reviews, which means people will not want to read your book. Any way you look at it, poor preparation will lead to poor book sales.

Not many of us have the luxury of hiring a professional researcher. Chances are you are reading this book because you have already written something and had no success with a trade publisher picking up your manuscript. Take the time to go over your manuscript carefully. Check your sources fully and then recheck them. It is very embarrassing to have a glaring mistake mentioned in a review or a letter from a reader. If you want to publish more than one book, you want to build up a cadre of fans of your writing such as Joe Garner did with his books. You do not want all of your fan mail to be full of corrections.

Non-fiction

It is often said you should find a niche and fill it. That's what I have done with this book. When I was researching about how to self-publish my first book, I discovered there is one nationally well-known book specific to Canada. I felt there was room for more. In the United States, there are well over fifty books on self-publishing that I could find. If you figure that Canada has about one-tenth the population of the U.S., it stands to reason there should be room for more books. Every writer has a different voice, different knowledge, and a different slant on how to present the material. That is one of the joys of writing. There are some excellent American self-publishing guides are full of material that is not country specific and, in fact, you should read several books on self-publishing before you start on your own venture. If you subscribe to the theory that you can never know too much you will only benefit from studying a multitude of resources.

Non-fiction is a very broad area, which is why trade publishers cannot publish every manuscript they receive. Writers often have a specific skill or have done some tremendous research on subjects of interest. If the writer fills a niche, it may be a small one. It may not lend itself to a short term marketable project that will carry itself financially. Publishers also hesitate to pick up work of unknown authors. Remember, trade publishers cannot afford to carry either a book or an author that is not paying its way. That is the reality of the business.

You might have knowledge or interest in a specialized topic. Your target audience may be small or select and you may think it is fine if you do not make the best seller list. If you are content to have steady sales over the long term, you might make an ideal candidate to self-publish.

How-to books

The how-to book is in the non-fiction category, but is more specialized. If you have a skill and want to share your knowledge with others, this is the category for you. *The Wealthy Barber* is a how-to book. So are many popular cookbooks. Interestingly, there is still a large market for cookbooks. To be properly illustrated they can be costly to produce, but look at the success of the *Company's Coming* cookbook series.

Let us say you are a great cook or woodworker or gardener. You can write and publish a book about the subject you specialize in. You would be considered a specialist in that skill and others might be interested in reading what you have to say. Take a minute now and think about the skills you have. Is there something that you seem to always be showing your friends or family how to do? Many traditional homemaking skills are popular. There never seems to be enough books about quilting, cross-stitch or knitting. If you have ever been asked to teach a class on something of this nature at your local school, it may be time for a book. Just be careful about the timeliness of the material. Crafts, especially, are a field where you have to make sure you are not behind the times, or your book will not sell.

You can often find how-to booklets advertised in the classified sections of magazines. This is a good place to test the response to what you have to offer. We will go into that in greater detail in a later chapter.

Family histories

The hobby of genealogy is growing almost daily. After spending much time and energy researching their family tree, many people want to put it into book form for the whole family to enjoy and keep. Self-publishing allows you to control the process so you will know exactly what the cost will be. Then you can pre-charge for the book so no one person is out of pocket while waiting for family members to pay for their copy.

If you have a special gift for storytelling, you might want to present your family history in that way. This could create a small local market in the community or communities your family has lived in. This would be especially true if your family was, if not prominent, but even moderately well known in a particular region. For example, your great-great-grandfather might not have been the Mayor, but he might have run a corner store for 25 years. This makes him part of that community's history as well as your own family's history. Handled properly, the history becomes the story of a man and his life or the story of several generations of a family. Allow your muse to be creative and you never know what you will come up with.

Regional Histories

Canada is jam-packed with fascinating history. Right now we are keen to learn about it too. This has produced a fairly sizeable market for regional histories. These could include the history of a neighbourhood, a town, a ghost town, or even a logging or mining camp. You might have grown up in a small town or ethnic neighbourhood whose story begs to be told. Your greatest sales will come within this community. You are more likely to have the local bookstore carry six copies than a large chain ordering 600. But regional histories have longevity. They are still selling a decade after you publish them. You cannot expect to make a large profit, but should be able to see steady long term sales.

Grants are available for writing books about

certain regions. Check *The Canadian Writer's Market* for all grants available in Canada. Many provinces provide grants to encourage history to be written. Of course competition will be tough, but it is worth a letter and a stamp.

Memoirs

Everyone has a story to tell. It does not matter if you are old or relatively young, you have a story. Many of our seniors who fought in one of the wars have written about their experience. People who have triumphed over a disease or a family tragedy are also writing about it. You, too, might have a story to tell.

Webster's Universal Dictionary defines *memoir* as: (n) an historical account based on personal experience; (pl) an autobiographical record. Often people read these to feel like they are not alone as they too go through experiences that only you can write about. That is one of the joys of a memoir. No two people will experience an event exactly the same way. That leaves a lot of room for this type of book.

Aside from the historical aspect of a memoir, there is the sharing of an experience. Perhaps you lost a parent as a child, had an alcoholic spouse or have successfully lived with a learning disability. When you write about your experiences and the emotions you went through at the time, others can empathize with you. Books like this often help others with the same problem. Many times people feel alone under adverse circumstances, and books help show them that they really are not alone.

The subjects I have mentioned here are not the only subjects that are popular for self-publishing. Humour, self-awareness, spirituality, cookbooks, fitness, and diet books are very trendy these days. There is no barrier to what you can write about. Any subject is acceptable and you can be successful if you follow the proper steps to producing a book.

TITLE

One of the best and worst things about self-publishing is that you get to make up the book's title. Usually, when a book goes to a trade publisher, the editorial department makes it up. I know writers who have not been happy about the chosen title, but they normally do not get a vote. Suffice it to say that if you want your book published, you often have to bite your tongue. This is not the case in self-publishing. It is part of the control you have over your material.

On the other hand, it can be a blessing to have a professional decide on your title. It is an art, and not one that comes naturally to all people. Take a look at the title of this book. I wanted it to be clear and leave no doubt what the book was about. Most books on self-publishing have the words in the title. In my case, I wanted book-sellers and readers to know this book is specific to Canada.

Sometimes titling a book is easy. Often it is not. And, unfortunately, a bad title can hurt a book's chances of being sold. The title should be fairly short. Try to keep it to five words or less. If your book is non-fiction, use a sub-title to give a clearer description of your book. Do not start your title with "Introduction to..." because thousands of books have that title and yours will not stand out. If your book is fiction or poetry, the title should tie into the theme. While this is not imperative, remember that you are just starting out and want to entice as many readers as possible. If you become a well-known author, you can use more literary license with your titles. Look at the publication *Books in Print* to see if the title you have chosen has been used for another book. While book titles are not copyrighted, you do not want the same title as another book or future purchasers might become confused.

The title is part of what a potential purchaser will look at in the seven seconds they spend on the front cover of your book. The working title you choose may seem very comfortable to you, but jarring to others. Brainstorm some title (and if necessary sub-title) ideas, and show them to people. Do not limit yourself to just friends and family either. Ask all kinds of people that you are acquainted with or do business with. If you really cannot come up with a title you are satisfied with, hire a professional to do it. This is too important to be left to chance.

PEN NAME

A pen name, or *nom de plume*, is the pseudonym an author uses to conceal their true identity. Often famous authors will use a pen name when writing in another genre than that which they are known for. Sometimes famous people will use a pen name because the do not want the book to be associated with what they do, or they do not want to use their fame to sell the book. Should you use a pseudonym? Probably not.

When you are an unknown author, you will only mask your identity. How do you expect to sell books if you do not give your real name? You want to garner fame and that will not be possible if no one knows who you really are. However, local people might recognize you and the word will get around, which could be embarrassing. In my experience, author/publishers tend to use odd pen names anyway. Your high school nickname is not likely appropriate. My advice is that unless you are already well known for something else, do not use a pseudonym.

EDITING

After you have written a manuscript, it

needs to be edited. There are basically two kinds of editing – content editing and copy editing. Content editing is the process of finding ways to make what you have written even better. It looks at the manuscript as a whole. Copy editing is the line-by-line and word-by-word search for errors in the text. Done correctly and methodically, editing will give your manuscript a professional look rather than one that advertises you as an amateur publisher. Professional editing will polish your book so it will hold its own with other books in the field that have been published by established trade publishers.

One of the drawbacks to self-publishing is that you do not have a professional trade publishing editor to help smooth out the rough spots or catch mistakes. If you can afford to hire one, this is the best route to go. Freelance editors advertise in publications like *Writer's Digest*, *Quill & Quire* or the Editorial Services section of *The Book Trade in Canada*. The Writer's Union and the Editor's Union of Canada offer editorial services. The editing will not come cheaply, but a good editor can really help showcase your best writing.

Many of us cannot afford an editor, so we have to look elsewhere. One place to start is the English department of your local high school, college or university. The teachers all have the education and training to assist you – some may even have the time. Colleges and universities might have English students who are willing to do the work for a reasonable fee in order to put the project on their resume. The cost is something you have to work out with a prospective editor. If you have received estimates from freelance editors, you will have some idea what the top end price is. Then figure out what you can afford. Some editors charge by the page and others charge by the hour. With the latter you have to be clear how long it will take for the editing job to be done. Make sure you make up a simple contract to ensure costs do not run over. And remember, this fee is tax deductible. Actually, you do not have to be a publisher to use the deduction. Full time writers can take advantage of editing deductions too.

If you are lucky and have a friend or family member who is well read, they might be willing to edit the manuscript for you. If you absolutely cannot find a teacher or professional, then this is the best option to use. When you do it this way, though, you must be clear as to what you want edited. Otherwise, ideas may clash and hard feelings flare up. If you feel you are being criticized, take the manuscript back. No book is worth losing friends over. I have one friend who only reads the manuscript for typographical errors and "the feel". I have her make a note in the margin if she encounters a section that is mentally jarring. You know what I am talking about – the part in a book that you reread because it did not seem to make sense. This way she is not expected to edit the content of my material, but helps me find rough spots.

Unless you have a great relationship, do not ask your spouse or significant other to edit your manuscript. Like friends, this can lead to hard feelings. You do not want to endanger your relationship over a book.

The other person who cannot edit your book is yourself. You are too close to the material. Having written and (I hope) rewritten the material, you cannot see it objectively. Every person who has self-edited has horror stories of things missed because they were the one who had written the original material. But, if there is no other choice, put the manuscript away for at least a month to distance yourself from it. Write other things such as poetry, short stories, or articles to clear your mind of the manuscript's topic. Then take it out and try to edit it.

You cannot rely on your computer's spell-checker or grammar checker either. Many people have, to their embarrassment, found simple mistakes when they counted on their technology. Spell checkers often give American spellings. If this is okay with you, do not bother to change the set up feature to Canadian English. Unfortunately, spellcheckers do not catch properly spelled words used incorrectly. For example, if you hold a key down too long and write *too* instead of *to*, the spellchecker will not pick it up.

You cannot rely on the grammar checker to

catch these mistakes either. The average grammar checker has formats for student compositions, business writing, and technical or scientific writing. None of these will work for you. It is time consuming to go through a whole chapter or manuscript. You may get frustrated that the grammar checker does not understand your writing style. It is a good place to start, but should never be considered the final editing.

Good old-fashioned reading is the only way to edit. Copy editing can be done by using a ruler and reading the text from the bottom of the page up to the top. Then you are not reading the material, but looking at it line by line and word by word. Copy editing needs to be done meticulously. It is time consuming, but it is time well spent. When you self-publish your manuscript you want it to look professional.

Before you publish your book, you have to remember that, first, you are a writer. You should have worked on perfecting your craft. Writing is not simply a matter of putting words on paper. It takes skill as well as dedication. If you have ever read an interview with a professional writer such as Stephen King, you will be aware that books are not written – they are rewritten. This is such an important point, you should make it into a sign and post it near where you write. My first book was completely rewritten three times. Each time it became a better book. Right now you are reading the fourth draft of this book.

You can take courses at your local college to learn how to write better. You can subscribe to *Writer's Digest* magazine for many how-to articles on various forms of this craft. You can get books out of the library. Simply look them up under *Subject: Writing*, take them home and read them. If you find any book that appeals to you, then buy it from a bookstore. The best way to learn about good writing is to read the works of good writers. Find at least three writers who have published in your field. For example, if you have written a regional history, read Pierre Berton's histories. If you are working on a memoir, then read the memoirs or autobiographies of others. When I am working on a book I do not dare get involved in reading a good fiction or I will not get to my computer. What I read for leisure are biographies. The richness of a good biography helps me find ways to convey what I want to say to my readers.

BOOK DESIGN

All books should follow the same design format. They have a front cover, preliminary material, text, back matter, and a back cover. Each part is an important element in the book. Your book will look amateurish if you do not follow the accepted format. A frequent problem with self-published books is that the new and unskilled author-publisher does not do enough homework to find out enough about book design. Never forget that your book is competing for shelf space against trade published books designed by professionals from all over the world. Attention to detail is critical.

FRONT COVER

Yes, you can tell a book by its cover these days. Potential readers will first look at the cover to determine if they want to select your book. An unattractive cover will not sell books. On the other hand, an attractive cover will not guarantee sales, but it will help tremendously. Studies show you have seven seconds to catch the attention of a prospective book purchaser. The cover is also critical in catching the attention of book review editors. A good cover is very important.

Unless you are an artist, and have some experience designing books, hire a professional. Cover design is an area where it pays to spend money. Look under *Graphic Designers* in the yellow pages of your telephone book. When you make contact, ask if the person has had any experience designing book covers. With those who respond positively, make an appointment to view their previous work. If you do not like what you see, go elsewhere. It is important that you never forget you are running a publishing business now. You have to make business-like decisions about your product. And some business decisions are hard to make. You cannot accept inferior packaging for your book. You will benefit from taking the time to find an artist who can produce a cover that will stand up to the competition on a bookstore shelf.

Do not think you will be able to find a good designer only in the large cities. I was able to find an experienced book cover designer in the small town where I live – with a population of less than 5,000. You will be surprised at the array of resource people you can find, even in smaller communities. With internet capability, many artists find they can live in a small community and e-mail or courier their work to customers.

BACK COVER

The back of the cover is as important as the front. Although many people simply look at the front cover, many more read the text on the back to see what the book is about. Take this book, for example. Did you look at the back cover to see what you might find inside? When you decide on a cover design, do not expect an artist to write the back cover blurb. That is your job. After all, you are the writer and should know best what is in the book. Spend time and ask others for their feedback on this. A poorly written back cover might lead a potential reader to believe the writing inside is poor, too.

Go to the library or a bookstore and look at

back covers of books similar to yours. In a notebook, jot down ideas that appeal to you. The text should begin with a short paragraph or question that acts as a *hook*. This is a strategy used in magazine and newspaper article writing that "hooks" the reader. Bullets are very popular as a way to list what is inside. Each bullet should have a tightly written short sentence following it. If you need to practice the art of rewriting, this is the place to do it. Make up several sample back covers and get opinions on which one works the best.

If you think it is relevant, put a short biography of yourself on the back cover. This should be no more than three sentences long. It should mention why you are an expert on the subject. If you are not, it could name any achievements that show why you were the best person to write this book. If you do not think a bio is necessary, then simply do not include it.

The subject reference also goes on the back cover. This tells librarians and bookstore owners in what section to place your book. You can use one, two, or three subjects. You can see on the back cover of this book it says *REFERENCE / WRITING*. That means it could be shelved in either of those sections in a bookstore or library. I chose Reference because many small bookstores do not have a specific publishing, or even writing, section.

At the bottom right of the back cover you will place your barcode. You can use either an ISBN bar or an EAN bar. Unless you have extra money to put into this project, you will find the UPC barcode too expensive. I will go into detail about barcodes in the next chapter. Place your book's price under the barcode. Often booksellers want their own price label on the book and this placement works best for them. Yes, you want to cater to what the booksellers want because they will hopefully put your books on their shelves.

PRELIMINARY PAGES

The preliminary pages or *prelims* are the pages of a book that you have before the actual text or body begins. They are numbered with a small Roman numeral, or have no page number at all. You can find any or all of the following pages:
* Book half title
* Series title, list of contributors, frontispiece, or blank page
* Title page
* Copyright notice, publisher's agencies, printing history, country where printed, ISBN, Cataloguing in Print (CIP)
* Dedication
* Table of contents
* List of illustrations
* List of tables
* Foreword
* Preface
* Acknowledgments (if not part of preface)

- Introduction (if not part of text)
- List of abbreviations or a chronology

Title pages

Some books begin with a half title page that only has the book's title written on it. There is no subtitle on this page, and it is usually set up very simply. The title is normally set near the top of the page with no other information on the page. This is an optional page. You can use a half title page if it fits into your budget.

The full title page will have the book's full title and subtitle on it, the edition if necessary, author, editor or translator's name, publishing company name and location, and the year of publication. If this is a new edition the number of the edition may appear on this page. It is customary to write *Edited by* or *Translated by John Doe* rather than *John Doe, Editor*. If you have an emblem or colophon (logo) for your publishing company, you would use it on this page.

Both the half title and title pages are on the *recto* or right-hand side of the page. This means you will have a blank *verso* or left-hand page between the two. If costs are tight and page count becomes important, it is not necessary to have a half title page. Then your prelims will begin with the title page.

Most non-fiction books should have a subtitle. That way you can give the book a catchy title and then explain more clearly what it is about in the subtitle. Subtitles are normally done in a different typeface and in a slightly smaller point size. This sets it off from the main title of the book. There is no colon or other punctuation mark to separate the two. Short titles are often done in a larger, bolder type to grab the public's attention. The subtitle can be half that size in either bold or regular type. You have to decide which looks better with the title. If the title is quite long, use a smaller type. This way it will not look crowded in the space. Try out different looks on a computer until you find the one you like best.

Frontispiece

The verso (left) page facing the title page can either be left blank or it can be used as a *frontispiece*. This is a decorative page that features a halftone (photograph) or line drawing relating to the overall theme of the book. Occasionally a short quote or line from a poem is included with the illustration on the frontispiece. It is not common, but can be done.

If the publisher chooses not to use an illustration in the frontispiece, this page can be used to list other books the author has published, other books in a series if this is part of a series, or other books on the same subject offered by the publisher. This page then becomes an *advertisement page*. If it is used as such, then you should use the same typeface as the book's body text. Make sure the book titles are a little larger than the *Other Books by...* line.

The best way to see how you want to set up your prelims is to go to the library and spend some time looking at books. They do not necessarily have to be about the same subject as yours, but try to keep it to the same type. For example, if you have written a history then look at histories and biographies. At least look at non-fiction in general. Get a feel for what looks clean and professional, and what looks plain gaudy. Take a notepad and write down things you like about other book's prelims. This will assist you in making your decisions.

Copyright page

The reverse side (verso) of the title page is the copyright page. The word copyright comes from two familiar words: copy and right. This page is also known as the *legal page*. Both terms describe it nicely. This page is important because it protects both the author and the publisher from illegal reproduction or other unauthorized use of the contents of the book. You do not want anyonc plagiarizing your material. That means they take what you wrote and put their name to it. Just as you should never do this yourself, you do not want others helping themselves to your work and taking credit for it. If anyone wants to quote you, the copyright page will give them information to get permission or give you credit for your work.

At the top of the page place the copyright symbol © along with the year of publication and your name. You can also use the word *copyright.* It is not necessary to have both, but most trade publishers still seem to prefer doing that. The symbol alone suits the copyright requirements of North America, most European countries, and many Asian countries. Beside your name print the phrase "All rights reserved". This ensures protection in most Latin American countries.

It is important to use the date the book is actually published. This is not necessarily the same date the book is printed. If the publication date is near the end or beginning of the year, this can be a difficult decision. But as long as the date is no more than one year off, it will not be a problem. A date that is more than a year off will have to be corrected. Pre-planning will help ensure this problem does not crop up.

Often there is a paragraph describing exactly what it is illegal to do with the book. Although not necessary, many publishers prefer to spell out just what a potential plagiarist cannot do. Of course, you could let someone take their chances in the court system, but ask yourself if you can afford to sue someone who uses your work without credit. This short paragraph ensures no one can claim they did not know exactly what a copyright means. It will tell them. If you want to register the copyright go to **www.cipo.gc.ca** and follow the instructions. At the time of printing, the fee was $65.00.

If this is not the first printing of your book, you should include the publishing history next. The year of first publication is first on the line, and the current edition is written beside it. To avoid having the printer completely reset this page, some publishers will include a line of consecutive numbers. They are set up left to right ranging from largest to smallest. This way the printer only has to delete the number of the previous edition. Otherwise you will print the edition number completely each time you put out another edition. If your book is realistically only going to be printed once, do not bother. If by some stroke of luck you get to print several editions of your book, you can use whichever method you prefer.

The name of the country where the book is printed **must** appear on the copyright page. Some publishers put it before the CIP information and some put it at the bottom of the page. It is a matter of choice. This information must also appear on the back cover or jacket. This way, the book is identified as a Canadian publication. If you have the book printed in another country, it will not be considered a Canadian book.

Some people who have self-published like to give a little free advertising for those who have supported them. You can print the name of the firm who designed the cover and/or who actually printed the book. Even though you have paid for their services, you might be pleased enough to include this information. But it is not necessary. In a trade publishing house, these things are done in-house, so they do not normally print it. Unfortunately, including the printer's name and cover designer also gives away the fact this is a self-published book. You might prefer, instead, to include these people in your acknowledgement.

In order to complete the copyright page, you have to have the CIP information. It is important that the information be placed on the page exactly as you receive it, including proper spacing and punctuation. You must put the ISBN on this page too. You do have the choice, though, of placing the ISBN either above the CIP information or beneath it.

The name and address of the publisher is printed at the bottom of the page. In trade publishing, the author's personal information is not given to the public – all mail goes through the publisher. Make sure you use the proper mailing address. This way if a reader wants to send a fan letter, they send it to the publisher. If someone wishes to quote from the book, they can request permission. If your publishing business address is also your personal address, you have two choices: you can use it with just the name of your publishing business or you can use a post box number. Be forewarned that using a post box number red flags a self-published book. This is one of those business decisions you have to make for yourself.

There are many setups for the copyright page. You can print all the information on the bottom half of the page, the top half of the page, or over the whole page. There is no set industry standard for this and it is simply personal choice. Look at copyright pages in books at the library and use a setup that you personally like.

Dedication

The first recto page after the title page is where you would place a dedication if you have one. Many authors dedicate their book to a loved one or in the memory of a deceased relative or historical figure. This is where you put your author's hat back on and dedicate your book to anyone you choose. It can be short or long. Again this is the author's choice.

The dedication page is usually in the same type and size as the body of the text. You can use any decorative element you want to make it a little fancier, but this is not commonly done. The most decoration you might find is a short dedication written in italics. The dedication is normally centred on the page with the first line about one-third of the way down. You do not sign the dedication because the reader already knows these are the author's words.

Epigraph

Some books contain an *epigraph*. This is a quotation pertinent to the book. As mentioned earlier, if space is at a premium, a short quotation can be put on the frontispiece. But normally it has its own page. If there is no dedication, the epigraph can be put on that page. If costs are getting high, and you really feel the book benefits from an epigraph, you can put it on the blank verso page facing the text or at the beginning of the first chapter.

An epigraph is done in the same text and size as the body, and is usually in italics. The source of the quotation is given on a line following the quotation. It is aligned right with no parentheses or brackets, although it can be preceded by a dash. If the author of the quotation is well known, you simply use the last name. If not, give the author's full name and the title of the work. You do not have to give bibliographical details for an epigraph.

Table of contents

The table of contents, or simply *contents*, is a very important part of the prelims. A potential reader will often open a book to the contents to see exactly what it contains. So you have to remember that this is part of the selling feature of your book. Do not "slap" it together. Give the contents a lot of thought and try out different designs. Readers use the contents to find their way around a book. It must be designed for ease of use.

The table of contents always begins on a recto page. It includes chapter numbers and names, and the page each chapter starts on. It also lists the page numbers for back matter such as the index, glossary, and any appendices.

Most new word processing programs and desktop publishing software can automatically make a table of contents from your manuscript. Make sure there is good contrast between the different parts of your contents. You may have divided your book into sections or parts as well as chapters. Each element should stand out distinctly from other elements. Never use all the same font type and size to create a table of contents. This not only shows your lack of experience, but it is difficult for a reader to use. Like other parts of book design, look at books in the library for models.

Lists

If you have written a technical or serious historical book, you might have several illustrations or tables you need to include. The easiest way for the reader to find them, or keep track of them, is to list them separately.

The list of illustrations comes first. It is titled simply *Illustrations*. The size and type of fonts should match the table of contents. It may be divided into sections such as Figures, Maps, etc. The title you give the illustration in the list does not have to be exactly the same title used for the actual illustration. It can be a simplified version. Normally, sections of photographs like you would find in a history book are not given in a list of illustrations. Sometimes your illustrations are inserted after the book is made up into pages and will not have a page number. When this happens you list it as *facing page 00* or *following page 00*. This enables the reader to find the nearest numbered page and look at the illustration.

The list of tables is placed next. If there is no list of illustrations, then the tables page is placed after the contents. Labeled *Tables*, it shows readers where they can find tables, charts, or graphs. Rules for design and numbering are the same as I have just detailed for illustrations.

Foreword

Try not to mistake a book *foreword* for the direction of forward. The one used in publishing is made up of two words – *fore*: first or in front of, and *word*: text. In order to make sure you do not misspell it, try to remember it is as the "first word". Which in effect, it is. It is an introductory statement written by someone other than the author. It can be a well known person or someone who knows about the subject of the book. It can be a few paragraphs long or can run into several pages. Regardless of length, it is done in the same type as the text of the book. The writer's name is placed at the end, often in caps and small caps, and it is aligned with the right margin. If the foreword is quite long, the writer's name may be given at the beginning instead of the end. Although many trade publishers include the place (institution or city) and the date, some style books discourage this practice. If you do choose to include it, this information is set flush left with a line between it and the text of the foreword.

Finding someone to write the foreword can be a bit of a challenge. You would normally write a letter to the person you want to write it and ask if they are willing. You should include a copy of the galleys if they are ready, or at least a copy of the manuscript. A person well known in a particular field will want to see the book before putting their name in it. A famous person will be hard to both track down and pin down. They get many requests for favours such as this. Do not let anyone charge you a fee for writing a foreword.

Having a foreword written can be an exercise in diplomacy. Sometimes the writer will do a great job. Other times you have to edit the text. And there are even times when you will be asked to write the foreword yourself for the writer's approval and name. Ideally you should give the writer a clear idea why you chose them. In a book about the history of a cadet summer training centre, I asked a retired Admiral to write the foreword because I knew he had been there as a young teenager and that he returned for his retirement parade. I saw it as a full circle and wanted him to write along that vein. It took several drafts to get it. But it did require a lot of diplomacy to deal with editing and rewriting. This is something experienced publishers deal with all the time so try to think about how they would handle it. This is the time when you put on your business hat.

If you think a foreword would enhance your book, look at other sources. It could be someone local who is knowledgeable about the subject. It could be someone you know who can tell why the book would be important to read. If you cannot find someone to write a foreword, leave it out. Instead you can write a preface.

Preface

The preface is written to explain to the reader why or how the author wrote the book. It can include the method of research if it is important, permissions for using previously published material, and acknowledgements. It should be kept fairly short – no more than one page. It is not necessary to have your name here because the reader will presume it is written by the author whose name appears on the title page.

Acknowledgement

If there is no preface, or if the list of people who helped get the book published is too long, a separate page for acknowledgements is inserted.

If the preface consists of little more than thank-you notes, an acknowledgement page would be used instead of a preface page.

As with the Introduction, Foreword, and Preface, the Acknowledgement page should be set up in the same type and size as the text in the body. The headings for these pages are normally done in a bolder type and can be one size larger. This is your choice. You can look at prelims in books in the library to see what you like. You can also try out different styles on the computer. Make sure you print out a hard copy so you get an accurate idea of what it looks like.

Introduction

In some kinds of books an introduction is necessary to provide background information. Material that is relevant to the book and needs to be read before the text, should not be put into the preface, but written in the introduction. It may be written by the author or another person with expertise on the topic.

If the introduction is a prelim, it is to be numbered in lower case Roman numerals. If it is going to be part of the text, it is numbered in Arabic numerals. If it is used to set the scene for the book, it should be considered part of the text.

Often writers confuse the *introduction* and the *preface*. Make sure you understand what each is and label them correctly. To do otherwise will indicate you are an amateur.

List of abbreviations

In technical books and some how-to books there might be a lot of unusual terms, abbreviations or acronyms for the reader to grasp. In this case, you include a list of abbreviations. If the list is one page it is placed on the verso page immediately before the text begins. If it is longer than a page, put this section in the book's back matter. Abbreviations are always listed in alphabetical order.

Editorial method

Scholarly books often include an explanation of the approach the author or editor has taken to the subject matter. If it is long, include it as a separate section. If it is short, and merely points out things such as word spelling or modernization of grammar, it should be included in the Preface.

List of contributors

When the book has contributions from several authors, you will include a list of contributors. It is most commonly set up in alphabetical order by author's surname. Their position or credentials are listed under the name. Sometimes a short biography is included.

Chronology

Historical books or novels have many characters and/or time periods in them. The best way to give the reader a clear understanding of events and characters as they appear is to include a chronology, designed so that the date is located along the left margin. The information is either placed at the right of the date or beneath it. It is best to put the chronology right before the text begins so it is easy to refer to. You can, though, put it after the text in the back matter. You also have the choice of having the whole chronology in the same type or making the dates bold. You have to decide which works best for your book.

TEXT

The preliminary pages should serve as a guide to the contents and nature of a book. The back matter provides reference material. Sandwiched in between is the *text*. Although not as extensive to design as prelims or back matter, it is the most important part of a book. It is, in fact, the book itself. Beginning as your idea, then created as a manuscript, the text is the body and soul of your book. We have already discussed the importance of producing your best writing, and having it carefully edited. Now you want to set it up to help, not hinder, the reader.

Chapters

Text is normally divided into *chapters*. You should already know where your chapter breaks are going to be. Although they do not have to be exactly the same length, they should also not be too noticeably different in size. Chapter titles should be fairly short and give a reasonable idea as to what is in the chapter. Remember, the chapter titles are what you use to make up your table of contents. Many potential book buyers check out the contents to see what the book is about. If your chapter titles are vague or cute, they will not convey the book's contents very well and you could lose sales.

Each chapter starts on a new page, ideally a recto page, if you can afford the extra few pages. But it is equally acceptable these days for a chapter to start on a verso page. A chapter has a *heading* also called the *chapter display*. It may include the chapter number, title, an epigraph (quote), and an author's name if this chapter was written by a different author. The chapter number can be centred, aligned left, or aligned right. It can be an actual number or the number written out. If you plan to write it out, make sure the page does not get too cluttered with the title. The chapter heading is normally set in a larger type style. The text of the chapter does not begin until part way down the page – at least a third of the way down is usually acceptable. Make sure all your chapter headings have exactly the same font, size, and alignment.

Occasionally a book will be divided into *parts*. This is most commonly found in historical fiction, multiple volume science fiction, or novels that encompass a large time span. Parts are also used in technical books, scholarly books, and large scale non-fiction books. It is recommended that the novice stay away from too many divisions, but use them if necessary to best organize your book. They should be designed to match chapter headings. The type of numbering should be identical as well as the font, size and alignment. You might notice during your research trips to the library or bookstore that some part headings look different than the chapter headings. Unless you have experience in using complimentary fonts, I do not recommend you try this. Stay with a simple, visually acceptable format. Take time to write the title for each part as you do for chapter headings. These too will be included in your table of contents.

Headings

In many non-fiction books, *headings* and *subheadings* are used to break the material into manageable lengths. You can see that I have done that in this book. It helps the reader find material more quickly. The chapter heading is a *major head* done in large, bold type style. A heading is a *minor head* done in a type style that is larger than the one you are using for the text of the book, but smaller than the chapter heading. Subheads tend to be a bold version of the text you are using. Do not get too carried away with heads and subheads or it will detract from the main message of the book. Make sure they are sufficiently distributed. If one chapter has several heads and the next only has one, it will look awful. It would be better to rethink the use of headings altogether.

At the top of every page in the book you will find *running heads*. They were named because they run across the top margin of the page. They can be used to identify the book title, chapter title, or section title. And I have even seen some that have the author's name. You have to decide which title you want to put in your running head. The most common two are either the book title on the verso page and the chapter title on the recto page, or the chapter title on all pages in that chapter. Again it is personal choice and is something you should look at on your trips to the library or bookstore when you research book design.

Epilogues and Afterwords

Part of the text, an *epilogue* or *afterword* allows the author to have a final word with the reader. It may encourage readers to find out more about the topic or pursue goals the book has presented. It may give the reader information on other books covering the same topic, although this can be accomplished with a list in the back matter. Epilogues and afterwords should be kept brief.

An author who wants to sum up the book topic would write a *conclusion*. More common in academic books, a conclusion can be fairly extensive and could take up as many pages as a chapter.

BACK MATTER

The *back matter* of a book acts as a reference section for the reader. This is where you put information that would help your reader to understand the text, but which was not really right for the text. Back matter may be made up of any of the following:

• Appendix
• Glossary
• Bibliography
• Index

Just because these sections are located at the back of the book does not mean they are not an important part of book design. They must be planned as carefully as prelims. Back matter is set in the same type style as the text, and numbered in Arabic numerals.

Appendix

An *appendix* is a section, or several sections, of a book that can give the reader data, explanations, elaborations, texts of documents, laws, survey questions and results, or long lists. The appendixes in this book mostly give lists of addresses. You refer to them when you want the information, but I have not cluttered up the text up with long lists of addresses. The appendixes are done in a smaller type style. You may think the plural *appendixes* is wrong, and that it should be *appendices*. According to the Webster's Universal Dictionary, they are both correct. You decide which term you want to use.

Glossary

The *glossary* is an alphabetical listing of terms used throughout the book, along with their definitions. It is commonly found in books that use unique or technical words. Because you may not be familiar with publishing or its terminology, I have included a glossary in the back matter of this book. Although you can define terms as they appear in the text, remember that back matter is used as reference. The reader can later refer to the glossary instead of looking up words in the text.

Each word or phrase is printed in boldface type. Sometimes it is italicized too. The first letter can be capitalized or the whole term can be in lowercase letters. It is important to remember that each definition in the glossary ends with a period, even if it is not a proper sentence. The text is all flush left with the margin. This means there are no indentations.

Bibliography

If you use other books or articles while researching your book, you must include a *bibliography*. A single list of sources is most commonly presented in alphabetical order. A lengthy list, or one from several sources can be separated into sections by subject or kinds of material.

There are many acceptable format styles to choose from. The most common one is the *flush and hang* style. This means that the first line of each entry is flush with the left margin while the rest of the entry is indented (or hangs). I personally prefer to use *The Chicago Manual of Style* as my model. Which ever style you decide to use, be consistent. Decide on the style guide you prefer and stick with it.

Index

A non-fiction book will be harder to sell without an *index*. Booksellers and librarians will look for one, and may not order your book if it does not have an index. It is the main reference that you provide for your readers when they need to find something quickly. Spend the time to do it right.

All pertinent words, phrases and names are included in the index. It is organized in alphabetical order by the first word. If the first word is *a, an* or *the*, you organize that phrase or title alphabetically by the second word. New word processing and desktop publishing software can do the job for you. Take a look at specific editing software on the market. If you do not have access to a computer, write each word or name on a separate index card and then put them in alphabetical order. As you set up the index, try to imagine what a reader might want to look up. When you are finished, look carefully at your list to make sure you chose important words. Do not make the index too long or too brief. You might want to ask someone to read the manuscript and make suggestions about concepts they find that need inclusion in the index. If you can afford it, consider hiring a freelancer to make up your indexes. Provide a copy of the typeset manuscript for them to work from.

Order form

You never find an order form in a book published by the trade book industry. The industry presumes if you want a copy of the book, you know enough to take the copyright page information to your local bookstore and order it. If you include a back matter order form, or even ordering information, it will be immediately apparent the book is self-published.

That said, it may help your sales to have an order form on the very last page of the book. David Chilton (*The Wealthy Barber*) was convinced to do this by a self-publishing consultant. The sales of his already successful book increased noticeably. This is one of those publishing decisions I mention periodically. Most books on self-publishing recommend that ordering information on the back page be included. If you choose to do so, it should be placed on the recto side of the last page in the book. Do not have it on the verso side of a page with text. This gives the reader a dilemma as to whether they want to cut up their book. I realize it could be photocopied, but as the publisher you want to make it as easy as possible for your book to be ordered.

Now you know how to choose a subject, edit the manuscript, and design a book. Sounds easy when I put it this way. But doing the work is not easy. It requires attention to detail and several trips to the library or a bookstore to do research. The goal is to give your book the most professional look you can achieve. To be successful, you have to think professionally. You do not have the luxury of sending the book to different in-house departments like a trade publishing house does. You are all those departments! Whenever you can afford to hire an expert, do so. It will make your job less painful. Before you make a design decision, ask yourself if it is going to help your book look more professional. Never forget, your book competes against professionally produced ones. Be prepared to spend the time, and the money if you have to, in order to give the competition a run for their money.

CHAPTER THREE
Make It Legal

A book is as individual as a fingerprint
– Sylvia Fraser
Novelist

GETTING READY

Now that you have a manuscript, and know how you want both the exterior and interior of your book to be designed, you need to get ready for the printer. Surprisingly, you have a lot of paperwork to fill out before you get to that stage. You cannot have the manuscript formatted until you complete the following steps. While you may sigh and wonder what all this has to do with self-publishing, you need to understand this chapter because it is integral to the publication of a saleable book. Without it, your chances of sales may drop to virtually zero.

COPYRIGHT

One of the first things new authors ask about is how to copyright their material. As I explained in the last chapter, it is not necessary to register the copyright in order to have protection in Canada. Many authors want to register their book, though, because they want the certificate that is issued. The certificate is evidence that your work is protected by copyright and you are the legal owner. Some authors think you should do it as a matter of course. Others believe that if your work is available only in Canada, or in your province, or even your local community, that the expenditure is unnecessary. Like many aspects of publishing, this is a personal decision.

The Canadian Copyright Office is in the Canadian Intellectual Property Office or CIPO in Ottawa. You can register either online or via regular post. The form is on the website at **www.strategis.ic.gc.ca**. The time it takes to register your copyright depends on whether any revisions or corrections are required. Under normal circumstances, you should receive your registration certificate within three to four weeks from the time the Copyright Office receives it.

It currently costs $65.00 to register a copyright. If there is an error on the registration certificate, there is no cost to issue a new one if the office made the error. If you did, then you have to pay another $65.00. Copies or extracts from the

Register, or copies of certificates or licenses will cost fifty cents per page. If you need a certified copy for some reason, the fee is $35.00 plus fifty cents per page attached.

ISBN

The International Standard Book Number identifies your book as a unique publication around the world. Each book, as well as each edition of a book, has its own ISBN. There might be other books in the world with the same title or another author with the same name as you, but the ISBN is unique. The ten-digit number allows booksellers to order books accurately and efficiently. Since computers are so commonly used in business, the ISBN has become essential. Most booksellers use some kind of database program, and books are entered by their ISBN rather than their title.

The ISBN for this book is 0-894208-00-5. The "0" or a "1" shows that the book originated in an English speaking country. For international purposes, Canada is considered to be English speaking. The block of six numbers identifies the publisher. In this case it identifies my company, Half Acre Publishing. The "00" tells us what title and edition of the book we are looking at and identifies it as a hardcover or softcover edition. In our example, this is the first softcover edition. The last number is a check digit – a mathematical function to make sure the rest of the numbers are correct. It ensures they have not been miscopied.

You order the ISBN from the National Library of Canada. There is no charge. Contact information is listed in the appendix. You can order individually or in blocks of 10 or 100. Unless you really plan to go into publishing full time, do not order more than the block of ten. The National Library is hesitant to give a small publisher more than a block of ten numbers anyway because, surprisingly, the publishing world is running short of numbers. To change the number of digits in the ISBN would cause drastic problems. So do not get a large block that you will not use. If you later decide to go into self-publishing in a big way, you can always order another block.

In order to be considered self-published, you are required to have your own ISBN. Being issued with a number from another publisher can cause unexpected problems. When I self-published my first book, the printer issued me with an ISBN from his block of numbers. Several orders have gone to his place of business because the publisher identification number is his, not mine. On one occasion a cheque, made out in his company's name, was even mailed to him, but for my book. We both had some bookkeeping to fix up after that. If someone offers to "issue you with an ISBN" I recommend you politely refuse.

Otherwise the book industry will consider that person to be the publisher. If it is someone you know well, or you would prefer not to have orders come to your home, then by all means accept an issued ISBN. Make sure you keep in contact with the person or company who issues the ISBN to you or you could miss out on orders or payments.

Subsidy and POD publishers will insist on issuing you with an ISBN. That means they are considered to be the publisher, not you. You cannot call yourself a self-publisher if your book is published by someone else. Reviewers will not even look at your book if it has the imprint of someone other than yourself. If the publisher moves or goes out of business, you will not know what has happened to your book orders. You are paying for your book and you are entitled to have your own little publishing company name on it. Of course, if you only want a small print run, and do not care if it will be sold, then accept an issued ISBN.

CIP

Cataloguing in Publication (CIP) is a voluntary program that catalogues Canadian books nationally and internationally before they are published. This cataloguing information is distributed right away to librarians and booksellers. It allows librarians, wholesalers, and booksellers to select and purchase new Canadian books. It is voluntary, does not cost any money, and is a great way to get your book introduced in the marketplace. Since it is used by the trade publishers, your book will look more professional.

You apply online at the National Library's website at **www.nlc-bnc.ca**. It is a matter of filling in the blanks. If the book has an introduction, preface, and/or table of contents, it can just be attached to the form. You might want to write down where the file is on your computer before you begin. Copies can also be mailed or faxed to the office listed on the website. The turnaround is quick so as not to hold up publishing schedules. Before you send it, though, you must make sure you know what subjects it should be listed under and have your ISBN number. If you have organized the publishing of your book properly, you will have your CIP in plenty of time to put the information on your copyright page.

The National Library has a new program called *New Book Service* that assists publishers to promote their books. The form is also online just below the CIP form. You include graphics and promotional text with this form. Some of the promotional material can include the foreword, a sample chapter, reviews, awards won, and information about readings. You can either e-mail it with the attachments or you can print and mail or FAX this information. You will require a JPG or GIF graphic file of your book's cover. It has to

■◆■ National Library Bibliothèque nationale of Canada du Canada	Canadiana Control No
CATALOGUING IN PUBLICATION INFORMATION • SEND WITH TITLE PAGE, INTRODUCTION, TABLE OF CONTENTS AND OTHER DESCRIPTIVE MATERIAL	Date Form Completed	Date CIP Data is required

Name Address and Phone No of Publisher	Which Imprint Will Appear on Title Page?

Name of Co-publisher (if any)	In-House Editor	Phone No

Authors Names and Functions (e g illustrators, editors) as They Will Appear on the Title Page

AUTHORS' FULL NAMES IF KNOWN	BIRTHDATE	CANADIAN CITIZEN	LANDED IMMIGRANT	NON-CANADIAN
		☐	☐	☐
		☐	☐	☐
		☐	☐	☐

Title and Subtitle

Edition Statement if any (e.g. 2nd edition, Canadian edition, revised edition)	Date(s) of Previous Edition(s)

Title, if Different, of Previous Edition(s)

IS THIS A REPRINT ☐ No ☐ Yes   DATE OF FIRST PRINTING?

IS THIS A TRANSLATION ☐ No ☐ Yes Please Give original Title | Date Published

Is this Publication Bilingual? (e.g. proportion of languages, 2 complete texts or text in one language plus summary in another)

Name the series (if any) as it will appear in the book	If Series is Numbered, the Number for this Title is
	ISSN for this Series

PROJECTED DATE OF PUBLICATION	Does Book Have		If a Multi-volume Work, How Many Volumes Are Planned?
Month Year	☐ Bibliography	☐ Bibliographical Footnotes	
	☐ Index		This Information is for Volume No.

What Type of Work is This? (e.g. novel, poetry, essays, biography, textbook)	Primary Audience (grade / age level or group for which it is intended)

IF BOOK CONTAINS PROCEEDINGS OF A CONFERENCE	Conference Number (if any)	Place	
	Name of Conference (if any)		Date(s) of Conference
	Will name of Conference Appear on Title Page? ☐ Yes	If Not, Where Will it Appear? (e.g. preface, introduction, cover)	

What is Primary Subject of Book?

(continue on separate sheet if necessary)

ISBN VARIATIONS	ISBN	Price
Where applicable, give ISBNs for different bindings of the same title, for different volumes of a multi-volume set or ISBNs of a co-publisher	ISBN	Price
	ISBN	Price

Name and Address to Whom CIP Entry is to be Mailed	DO YOU WISH YOUR MATERIAL TO BE RETURNED? ☐ Yes ☐ No

NL/BN 41/97   FRANÇAIS AU VERSO   Canadä

Figure 1

be no larger than 72 pixels per inch and the longest side cannot be larger than nine inches. You can use a PDF file for the text. Make sure the whole package is no larger than 200 kilobytes. The service is a free of charge and can be very beneficial to any publisher, but especially small self-publishers. It is worth taking the time to submit your listing to the New Book Service.

CANADIAN BOOKS IN PRINT

Once you have an ISBN and a CIP, you can register your book with *Canadian Books in Print*, a publication that is put out once a year. This information is also included in the Fall Announcements section of *Quill & Quire,* which is a subject-arranged and indexed listing of new Canadian books. It is easy to submit an entry and will cost you nothing. You only have to fill out the Publisher Listing Form once. You include it with the CBIP Title Entry Form for the first book you publish. After that, you will receive a printout once a year to confirm that you still wish to be listed. When you enter any books in the future, you then only have to send in a Title Entry Form.

Self-published books are eligible to be included whether they are published by an individual, group, or association. They must, though, be available to the public. That means your family history would not be eligible if it is printed

Canadian Books in Print Title Entry Form
Quill & Quire Fall 2001 Announcement Form

(For CBIP use)
Entry:
Code:

If eligible, information from these forms will appear in **Canadian Books In Print**, 2002 edition, and in *Quill & Quire's* **Fall Announcements**, September 2001 issue. Please read enclosed CBIP 'Instructions for Publishers.'

■ Only books published between July 1 and December 31, 2001 are eligible for inclusion in *Quill & Quire's* **Fall Announcements**.
■ Use this form, a photocopy or a facsimile, to submit all titles, whether forthcoming (to *Quill & Quire* and CBIP) or missing backlist (to **CBIP** only).
■ Please type or print CLEARLY, complete the entire form, and **return BOTH copies, plus enclosed printout, by June 15, 2001.**
■ Return to: Canadian Books in Print, University of Toronto Press, 10 St. Mary St., Suite 700, Toronto, Ont. M4Y 2W8.
■ Inquiries: Marian Butler, Editor, Tel: (416) 265-1631, Fax: (416) 921-6353.

1. Title _____

2. Subtitle _____

3. Author(s) For collections, give editors with the notation (ed.)   (1) _____
                                                                              surname   given name(s)

    (2) _____   (3) _____
         surname   given name(s)   surname   given name(s)

4. Illustrator(s) The illustrator is ☐ an artist ☐ a photographer

    (1) _____   (2) _____
         surname   given name(s)   surname   given name(s)

5. Translator(s) (1) _____   (2) _____
                      surname   given name(s)   surname   given name(s)

5a. Is at least one of the above people (author, illustrator, translator) Canadian? ☐ Yes ☐ No

6. Price $ _____ hardcover $ _____ paperback $ _____ other
                                                                                              (please specify)
7. ISBN _____ hardcover _____ paperback _____ other

8. Number of volumes (if more than one) _____ vols.   9. Number of pages: _____

10. Number of illustrations _____ b&w _____ colour Illustrations are ☐ located throughout the book ☐ in separate section(s)

11. Series _____

12. Edition: check one or more of the following as appropriate:
    ☐ Appearing for the first time in any format
    ☐ Previously published but now appearing in paperback
    ☐ Being reprinted. Previous printing was in the year _____
    ☐ A revised edition   ☐ An annual (in either case, indicate the extent of the revisions under no. 13 below)
    ☐ Other (please explain) _____

13. Description (about 30 words; not required for textbooks or new paperback editions of previously published books)
    _____
    _____
    _____
    _____

14-16. Audience: Check one or more of the following as appropriate:
    ☐ Trade book (i.e., will be sold in trade bookstores)   ☐ Scholarly
    ☐ Textbook (indicate academic level) _____   ☐ Technical/professional
    ☐ Children's or young adult (give age level) _____ ☐ Self-published

17. Publisher _____
    Address _____
    Is this a co-publication originating outside Canada? ☐ Yes ☐ No   Is CIP available? ☐ Yes ☐ No

18. Publication date Year _____ Month _____

19. Subject(s) (1) _____ (2) _____ (3) _____

20. Forms completed by: _____ Phone: _____

Figure 2

only for your family. If the author makes any financial contribution to another publisher toward publishing costs, it is not eligible. In other words, if a subsidy publisher puts out your book under their company's name and imprint, you cannot have it listed in CBIP. Since you have gotten to this chapter, I will assume you are hoping to self-publish your book and this problem will not come up.

To be eligible, a book must be published in Canada and carry the imprint of a Canadian publisher. Once you start your self-publishing business, you will be a Canadian publisher (see Chapter 5). The book has to be 49 or more pages long. Exceptions will be made if a shorter work is poetry, children's literature, or books for people just learning how to read (called *new literates*). Maps, calendars, sheet music, prints, newspapers, periodicals, looseleaf services, catalogues, microfiche, photocopies, portfolios, audiovisual material, and computer software are not eligible. To receive the forms from *Canadian Books in Print*, contact:

Canadian Books in Print
University of Toronto Press Incorporated
10 St. Mary Street, Suite 700
Toronto, ON M4Y 2W8

ADVANCE BOOK INFORMATION

The R.R. Bowker Data Collection Centre is an

American company that puts out several important directories a year. Among them is one called *Forthcoming Books in Print*. Even though this is not a Canadian directory, it is used by booksellers throughout North America. They also put out *Books in Print Plus Canadian Edition,* which is specific to books published in Canada. Like the CBIP, it costs nothing to have your book listed.

In order to have your book listed, you need to use the BowkerLink Publisher Access System. Go to **www.bowkerlink.com** and click on *Add / Update in Books in Print and Publishers Authority Database*. Then click on *Register*. You have to read the statement of use and click on *I Agree* if you wish to register. Follow all instructions and your username and password will be e-mailed back to you to be validated. This might take up to three business days.

Although R.R. Bowker prefers to receive bibliographic information online, you can still use the old fashioned fill-out-the-form method. The Advance Book Information form is commonly called the *ABI* in the industry. It is easy to fill out and includes a guide explaining what each line requires. You need to order one from R.R. Bowker well in advance of your book's print date. Note that this is for *advance* information. But do not panic if you are under a tight deadline. You can still send in the ABI to be included in the Canadian edition.

After you have filled out the form, make

several photocopies. You can include them in your media packages that we will discuss in Chapter Six. The information required on the form gives details about your book. Any distributor, publicist, or reviewer will be grateful for that. It will also give your book a better chance at being read by these people. R.R. Bowker is also open to receiving any press releases or advertising brochures you have for your book. Send information to:

R.R. Bowker
630 Central Ave
New Providence, NJ
USA 07974

Do not forget to use enough postage on the envelope to send it to the United States or it will be returned to you.

LEGAL DEPOSIT

Since 1953, when the National Library of Canada was created, Legal Deposit has been in effect to ensure books are accessible to present and future generations. A depository of all new Canadian books, the National Library administers legal deposit as part of its responsibility to preserve Canada's published heritage.

Each Canadian publisher is required to send copies within one week after the book's release. How many you send depends on how many you produce. If you make 101 or more copies of your book, you must send two copies to the National Library. If you make more than three and less than 101 copies, you are only required to send one copy. If you publish less than three copies, you do not have to send anything. Copies of books sent to legal deposit are a deductible expense on your taxes, as well the postage paid for sending them.

Publications received by legal deposit are catalogued and listed in *Canadiana*, the national bibliography which is circulated in Canada and other countries. Sometimes the books are the subject of public readings and author book signings as part of the National Library's public program events. When you bundle up your book(s) to send, there is a form to include. You can request it when you order your ISBN and CIP from the National Library.

BAR CODES

If you turn this book over you will see a bar code on the back cover. It is used to identify this book when retailers run it past their scanners at the cash register. These are the days of technology, and this is how retailers keep records of products and prices. There are three kinds of bar codes with different needs and different costs. You will have to decide which one is best for your book.

The most common bar code found on books is the *Bookland EAN* code. This conforms to the

European Article Numbering system. The EAN numbers are at the bottom of the block. The *9 78* means this product is a book. The rest of the number is the book's ISBN number with different last, or check, digit. Sometimes the ISBN is also listed at the top of the block. The EAN bar code is used in bookstores only, including the large chain stores. A digital version will cost in the $11 to $25 range.

You have the option of ordering an EAN bar code with an add-on block that is smaller than the EAN bar code and is situated to the right of it. This add-on can be coded with the book's price or title. When you order your bar code, discuss your needs with the company you order it from. Bar codes can be ordered from some printers or book packagers. Otherwise there are bar code companies listed in the appendix. You can use barcode software if you feel comfortable with that. You can find software on the internet. It should cost no more than having a company make it though. Usually the software prints barcode labels. I would recommend if you want the code printed directly on your book cover, have it made professionally.

The type of bar code you might be most familiar with is the Universal Product Code or UPC. This block is on pretty well everything we purchase these days. If you want your book to sell in grocery or department stores, you will need the UPC bar code. But it is expensive. The activation fee was $245 in 1998, and there is an annual membership fee. The total cost can now run over $1100. Whether this is a worthwhile expense depends on the book you have written. If you imagine a huge market for the book, it might be worth your while. The best thing to do is ask for advice from your distributor or wholesaler. They will know where they plan to sell your books. If you decide not to use a UPC and your book becomes a best seller, you can always have it put on future print runs.

The third kind of bar code is a simple ISBN code. It is acceptable in small, privately owned bookstores. It usually costs the same as an EAN bar code so you might as well order one of those. Remember, one thing we are striving to do is make our book look professional. An ISBN bar code or no bar code at all screams "amateur".

The bar code goes on the lower right side of the back cover of a softcover book. If you are publishing a hardcover book, it should be placed on the top of the left hand flap of the dust cover. If you are still unsure where to place it, go to the library or bookstore and have a look at books there. Correct placement of the bar code is another way to make your book look professional. If you have any questions, do not hesitate to ask experienced distributors or trade publishers. And if you have printed a book without a bar code, you can still order packages of stickers. Mind you, it is quite a chore to attach 500 or 1000 stickers to your books, so try to plan ahead.

PRICING THE BOOK

At this time you have to decide on the cost of your book to the consumer. You will be asked for this information on many of the previously discussed forms. It is a fairly tough decision. You want to price it so you make money from the book, but ensure the price is not so high that no one will want to buy it. You want to make sure you are making a reasonable profit from your business venture or you will not feel encouraged to do it again. There is no reason why you should have to support your self-publishing like it was a hobby. You might not make a lot of money, but you should at least make enough to pay for the product and your time.

Interestingly, if you price a book too low you actually harm your chances of selling many books. In the publishing industry there is a fair market value put on books. This price is determined by several factors such as size, length, and product cost, among other things. If you price your book too low, potential readers might wonder what is wrong with it. You also cut into your profit. This profit is necessary to promote and publicize your book. If you do not have enough money to do this, you will see sales dry up. Too many new author-publishers price their book too low, thinking it will sell more quickly.

Do not forget that book purchasers are shrewd consumers. They love books, are willing to pay a reasonable amount for books, and know what books are worth. Do not insult the intelligence of your potential buyers. You are the one who will suffer in the end.

So just how does one actually price a book? The obvious answer is to figure out the production cost and multiply it by the industry standard for pricing. There is a set industry standard which most self-publishers know nothing about. Of the three best books on self-publishing I found recommendations for pricing as varied as "4-5 times", "5-8 times", and "not less than 8" times the production cost. One author even suggested that mail order how-to books run 10-20 times production cost. How is that for variation? In Canada, trade publishers use a formula to determine the cost of a book:

F (fixed cost) + V (variable cost) = Production cost
Production cost / Print run = Unit cost
Unit cost x cost factor (4,5,6) = Cover price

So how do you figure this out? Fixed costs remain the same no matter how many books you print and can include editing, cover design and typesetting. Variable costs are those that change with the size of the print run and can include paper, printing costs, and cost of binding. You add these costs up and divide that amount by the number of books you plan to produce. This gives you the exact cost of producing each book or *unit cost*. Canadian publishers multiply the unit cost by either 4, 5, or 6 to get their *markup*. So how do you know which factor to use to determine the markup of your book?

The first thing you have to determine is the number of pages in the printed book. The total page count includes prelim and back matter. Your print costs will also be strongly influenced by total page count. Then go to your favourite bookstore and find books with the same (or close to) page count, same number of colours on the cover, and similar subject matter. This will give you a ballpark idea of the minimum price that books like yours are selling for.

The next step is to figure out the expenses involved with producing your book. You want to include editing, typesetting, design, cover, and printing costs as well as advertising and marketing costs. If you do not have all these costs figured out yet, now is the time to do it. You will need to get printer's estimates and decide which one you will accept. When the time comes to set the price for your book, you have to put on your "business hat" and pull all the information together to make an informed decision. After you have calculated all costs involved in the production of the book, divide the total by the number of books you intend to print (the print run) to reach the unit cost. Then multiply that number by 5 (the markup). See how it stacks up against the books you have looked at in the bookstore. Decide if you have to adjust the price lower or higher. If it is within a dollar of other books, you should be okay. Unless you are planning to specialize in educational publishing where the mark up is usually 8, you should use 4,5, or 6 as your markup number.

Do not choose a price that is an even amount. The "rule of .95" is the rule of consumerism. If your book is worth about $15.00, price it at $14.95. Even though consumers are more savvy, many studies show that this strategy still works. The only time you should consider using an even number for the price is if you are marketing solely by mail order.

When you total up the cost to produce your book and you find you can only charge two or three times the cost, you have to go back to the drawing board for some more hard decisions. If your printers' estimates are not too similar, you might want to go with a less expensive printer. Perhaps you can shorten the page count. This is done by either doing some serious editing or making the font size and leading smaller. Another way is to use cheaper paper, take out some illustrations (especially photographs), or change the colour count for the cover from four to two. This exercise will give you a greater appreciation for trade publishers who have to do this kind of thing all the time. If you cannot make money with an industry mark up, you need to rethink the whole project. Booksellers know the value of books and will not buy something too high-priced to sell.

PUTTING IT ALL TOGETHER

Once you have collected all the information you need, it is time to have your book formatted. Although I go into this in more detail in the next chapter, you need to be careful about where you place such information as the CIP in the book. If you hire someone to format for you, they will have their preference. Make sure it synchronizes with your preferences. You should now be carrying the idea in your head of how you want your book to look.

As you can see now, a lot of information is required before you can even have your manuscript turned into a galley. During this process you have to remember to think like a business person. Unless you have to edit for length, the writer part of you must be tucked away. You are on the track to becoming a self-publisher and have to keep that in mind at all times. If you are still a bit emotionally too connected to your manuscript, perhaps you should put it away for six months and wait until you feel ready to view it in a businesslike manner. Write something else to get it out of your head. Then take it out when you feel you can publish it less emotionally and are ready to view it as a commodity to be sold.

Never lose sight of the fact that you want your book to be professional in appearance so it can compete for shelf space with other publishers. You will need to distance yourself from your book as something you poured your soul into. You need to think of it at a product to be sold. If any of you have had experience selling anything in your lifetime, you know you sometimes have to make tough decisions in order to make a sale. It is no different in the publishing industry.

CHAPTER FOUR
Building a Book

*The purpose of art is the lifelong
construction of a state of wonder.*
                                    – Glenn Gould
                                        Pianist

TYPESETTING

Typesetting is an old publisher's technical term for *formatting* your manuscript. Before computers were invented, individual letter forms made of lead had to be set by hand before a book could be printed. Today this is done on the computer and either printed out for offset printing or saved to a disk for digital printing. Whichever type of printing you choose, your book interior has to be properly designed in order to look like a book. A complete description of everything that should appear between the covers of a book was given in Chapter Two. In this chapter you will learn the technical specifications for designing a book interior.

Right now your manuscript is probably on 8-1/2"
x 11" paper (and preferably double spaced). But it
could be handwritten or even single spaced. If you
have done it on a computer, the next step will be
easier to accomplish. What you need to do now is
have your manuscript formatted so it looks like a
book. This is optimally done with a desktop publishing program like PageMaker or QuarkXPress
or InDesign. While you can format your manuscript in a good word processing program, it is better to use DTP software. And I recommend you
never format as you write your book. Since all
good books are rewritten rather than written, formatting as you write would require a tremendous
amount of technical changes each time you make
written changes, eating up a lot of time. Write
first, and format after it is completed and edited.

YOU OR AN EXPERT

Another big decision you have to make is who
will typeset your book. In order to answer this question, you need to answer some important questions:

1. Do you know how to format on your computer
   using your word processing program?
2. Are you skilled in the use of a good desktop publishing program?
3. Do you know how to make an index on your
   computer?
4. Do you know the elements of design of the interior of a book?

In Chapter Two, I described all the parts of a book's interior. How well did you understand it? Do you have an eye for design? If you are uncertain, you need to take your manuscript to someone who can format for you. Usually it will be a desktop publishing firm or typesetter. As with others whom you will do business with, make sure the firm has experience with books. And look at samples of their work. Some firms may have done several books, but not very well. They have a sort of "template" they use and that is what you get. Ask for two or three proofs and do not accept anything less than a professional job. Take a book, either from the library or one you have purchased, and show the firm exactly what you want. There is no copyright on interior book design so you can copy something you like. It will cost you to have a company format your book, but this is some of the best money you will spend on making your book ready for the reading public.

DOING IT YOURSELF

If you plan to do the typesetting yourself, you need to be aware of a few industry standards. Margins are something most self-publishers do not pay attention to. Unfortunately for them, the white space is as important as the text. This is what is "pleasing to the eye", so to speak. If there is too little white space, it can actually cause anxiety to the reader. This is part of the psychology of reading. I will not go into detail on that here. Just suffice it to say that in the industry white space should account for close to 50% of the book. Art books and highly designed books may have as much as 75% white space. You can save money by having smaller margins, but you may lose money in the long run when your book with the crowded text does not sell. Remember, all money is made from the finished product.

You want to arrange the text on facing pages so it is seen as a unit. Book margins are similar to magazine margins. The narrowest margin on the page is the gutter. At the same time, the combined gutter of both pages is wider than the other margins. The margin at the top of the page is larger, increasing more on the outside edge, and increasing the most on the bottom of the page. Confused? Take a ruler and measure the margins in this book. You will see the gutter on this page is 1", the top margin is 3/4", the outside edge margin is 3/4", and the bottom margin is 5/8". Each one is larger than the other. Make sure the gutter margin is large enough so that the text does not disappear when the book is bound. It is better to adjust font and leading size than be too cheap with the margins.

TYPOGRAPHY

The title page and the first page of each chapter are your showpieces. Make sure they are

placed on the recto side of the page. Some publishers are spreading the title across both pages.
While this can be dramatic, be careful that it
looks that way and not just silly. Type (or font)
for the chapter headings is normally the same
type used for the text. You also have to decide
how you want to begin your chapter. Some books
have a fancy initial letter, which can be in a different font. Some do not indent the first paragraph of the chapter while others indent halfway
across the page. You might want to start the
chapter a third or even half-way down the page.
Decide what looks best for your book.

While headings should be larger than the
text, they should be no larger than 18 to 24
points. A small type heading surrounded by
white space can be as dramatic as a large size
type heading. Subheads should be close in size to
the text. To distinguish them, try putting them
in all caps, bold face or italics. Also try to keep
headings from being too close to the bottom of
the page and have no less than three lines of text
below a subhead. At the same time, try to have
no less than two lines above a subhead at the top
of a page.

How you want running heads or titles and
page numbers to appear is another exercise in
decision making. You want to make it easy for the
reader to always be aware of the book's title, the
chapter title, and the page number. In non-fiction, the book title traditionally goes on the left

hand page while the chapter title goes on the right. I chose this method, but could just have easily had the chapter name on both pages, or the book title on both pages. It was my decision. I used .5 size lines for my running head. There is no requirement for a line unless you think it benefits the interior design of your book. And remember that you do not often see running heads or titles in a fiction book. What you do see, if you want some kind of running head, is the author's name. While it does not matter if your page number is at the top or bottom of the page, put it in the outside margin of the page. If it is a small book, such as a poetry chapbook, you can centre it on the bottom of the page. Page numbers detract from the text if they are centred on the top of the page.

Do not use a print size smaller than 10 point. If a book is long and you want to keep the page count down, this is the way to go. On the other hand, if your book is shorter than you would like, use a larger typeface and more leading (the space between the lines). This book was set at 12 point New Century Schoolbook with 15 point leading. Make sure your leading is no more than 1 to 3 points in size. Space between words is usually 1/4 em and no more than 1/3 em. You want your readers to enjoy reading your book and not feel overwhelmed by either too much text or too small sized text on a page. Set your justification at *full* so the text fits nicely between the margins. A decent desktop publishing program will hyphenate automatically.

FONTS

The font is the type of letters you use to write your text. There are two major subdivisions in font type: *serif* and *sans serif*. The main feature of a serif font is the cross strokes at the line ending of each letter. Some people think serif fonts have little "tails" on some letters. A sans serif font like Arial has no cross strokes. Serif fonts are generally considered to be more readable than sans serif fonts. As already noted, the text in this book is New Century Schoolbook.

Many types of serif fonts are used in book design. The most commonly used fonts in the Canadian publishing industry are Baskerville, Bodoni, Century, Garamond, and Times Roman. You should be familiar with the latter since it is the default font in many word processing programs. Other acceptable fonts are New Century Schoolbook, Palatino, and Bookman. While they are all serif fonts, they do have different characteristics. The best way to determine which one you think would look best for your book is to print a page in each of the fonts you are considering. Make sure the page is printed with the margins and headings you have chosen. This will give you a realistic idea of how it will look on a page in your book.

PRINTING PROCESS

Like many other products, a manuscript has to go through a process before it becomes a book. Traditionally, books are printed on good paper and covered, or *bound*, in one of several ways. Books come in many cut sizes and their pages can come in different weights of paper. They can be bound in cloth, paper, or even plastic. You should have made these design decisions by now or have a good idea what you want. If you have not, take time to complete this step of the publishing process before you approach a printer. Printing is the most expensive part of producing a book and you need to ensure you make good decisions about your printing. A bad decision can cost thousands of dollars and leave you with a book that is not easily marketed.

By now your manuscript should have been edited, revised, designed, and formatted. You should have a camera-ready copy, and either a PMT or a digital copy of the cover. You are now finally ready to have your book printed. If you are one of those people who excels at multi-tasking, you would have been looking for a printer while you were having the book typeset. Just keep in mind that submitting your book to a printer is only possible if you have had enough typesetting done to be sure of your page count. Printers cannot give you an estimate if they do not know exactly how many pages it will be and what kind of cover it will have. They also need to know if there will be illustrations or any colour on the inside. And finally, they need to know how many colours your cover will be printed in. That is a lot of things for you to have sorted out before you even approach a printer. At the same time, you cannot finish filling out some legal forms because you need to know how much your book is going to cost. The total amount is necessary to determine how much you will charge for it. As you can see, several things are tied into each other. Without one, you cannot have the other. Take the time you need right now to make sure you have covered all the necessary steps to be ready for the printer. If you make a mistake now, you can fix it. If you discover a mistake after the books are printed, you are stuck with them.

PRINTERS AND ESTIMATES

Before you have your book printed, you will need to get printers' price quotes from at least three different printers. Even if you live in a small community with only one printing firm, get several quotes from nearby communities. If it becomes necessary to have your book printed out of town, and your books shipped, do not hesitate to do so. Several books on self-publishing tell you to get quotes from as many as 25 printers. That is your choice. While it may be necessary in the United States, it is not necessary in

Canada. We have far fewer printers here. Three, or four at the very most, will be sufficient.

You want to have your books printed by a *book printer*. A printing firm whose business is mostly made up of producing business cards and letterhead will not normally have either the knowledge nor the equipment to handle book print runs. Furthermore, if your first print run sells well, you need to be working with a printer who not only understands, but can handle, getting another one done in a timely fashion.

Figure 1 is a sample of what a printer's quote should look like. Make up the forms on your computer and print off as many as you need. Fill in the details about what you require as completely as possible. If a printer tells you all that information is not necessary, let them know that you really do require all that information. Do not be put off. If you get the sense a printer is not taking you seriously, take your business elsewhere. Remember you are a business person now. And your business is getting your book published.

In traditional offset printing, the more books you have printed the lower the cost. This is not as simple a statement as it seems. If you have used the formula to price your book accurately, you will know how much you can spend to have it printed and still make profit. A reasonable print run by a self-publisher in Canada is 500-1000 books, but 250-300 is quite acceptable too. A second print

REQUEST FOR QUOTATION
Half Acre Publishing
7311 Bell McKinnon Road Duncan BC V9L 6A8
Phone/FAX (250)-746-3919 halfacre@selfpublishing.ca
www.selfpublishing.ca

BOOK TITLE: Self Publishing in Canada: A complete guide to designing, printing and selling your book.

QUANTITY: prices for 1500

TOTAL PAGES: 288

TRIM SIZE (Includes front and back material): 5.5" x 8.5"

PAPER: TEXT: 50#
                COVER: 12 pt

ARTWORK: 7 line illustrations - no photos

COVER: 4 colour

BINDING: Perfect binding with laminate

FORMAT: Disk (program?) or camera ready

FEE FOR EXTRA PAPER COVERS:

PACKAGING:

SHIPPING CHARGE:

DELIVERY DATE:

RE-ORDER TURNAROUND TIME:

DROP SHIP CHARGE:
     MINIMUM NUMBER:

TERMS:

Over/under run not to exceed 10%.
Boards, flats, and all artwork will be returned to the customer upon completion of project.

This quote good for 14 days from date shown below.

Signed _____

Date _____

Figure 3

run does not cost nearly as much to produce since your book is already set up. Even though the estimate will indicate in hard numbers that larger printings are less costly, how much do you save if you end up with one or two or three or five thousand unsold books in your basement or garage? It is better to spend a few more pennies up front and not have to worry about storage – especially long term. Do not be miserly or you could end up regretting your decision to self-publish at all.

TYPES OF PRINTERS

Today there is a wide variety of types of printers. You can have a large book run done at an offset printer or have your book printed one at a time by a print-on-demand (POD) printer. You can even have it photocopied on very sophisticated and expensive machines. Some use ink and some use laser. Others do not even use paper - your book is online. It can be very confusing for a first time publisher. You need to find the printer that best suits your needs and those of your book. While you should ask advice of others who have gone the self-publishing route, do not let their views sway you. After all, this is your book and you know best how to present it to the world. I know two people who have had books printed by a POD printer that I would not give a dime to. And yet they were happy with the result. At the same time, they would not go near an offset printer. Take your time at this step and do your homework. Printing is where most of your money goes and you do not want it wasted.

Offset Printers

Most books have been published by offset printing since World War II. First, you must make sure your manuscript is *camera ready*. This is done at the time of typesetting. The copy must be on high-grade paper and can be either laser printed or printed with a good quality inkjet printer. For the latter, use a high dots-per-inch (dpi) and the darkest black ink. The best thing to do is to put a new ink cartridge in the printer to ensure the clearest colour. Print all of the pages at the same time so there is a consistency to the print. Otherwise you could end up with some pages having darker text than others.

The offset printer takes these pages, photographs them, and makes a negative of them. Thin plates are made and bent over cylinders or drums. The text and illustration images are then etched into the surface. The ink will adhere to the etched areas only. Next to this drum is another one that is covered with a rubber blanket onto which the plate *offsets* the images. The rubber covered drum rolls against the paper and prints on it.

Many books on self-publishing advise you to have metal plates made and then keep them for reprints. Today most printers use disposable plates (called *silver*) that are meant to be used only one time. The cost should be no higher than for metal because this method is actually less expensive. Discuss this with your printer. If your chosen printer does use metal plates, make sure it is clear in your contract that the plates are your property.

Offset printing is the way trade publishers make books. They either have their own press or contract out to a large professional firm that specializes in book printing. Some have whole departments to handle this fairly technical aspect of producing a book, but you have just yourself and the printer you decide to hire. The best bet is to try and find a printer who specializes in books rather than flyers, business cards, and stationary. The latter may not be helpful to you because books are not their specialty. And do not be afraid to have your books printed in another city or even another province. If there is no one in your region who can do a professional job, you might have to go elsewhere. Never take a chance that your book will look amateurish. It will make it harder to sell.

Ask your printer questions about the process they use. Have them go over any part of the sequence that you do not understand. Do not be intimidated if they seem impatient. This is the largest outlay of money for a self-publisher and you have every right to know exactly how it is being spent. You should have with you the printers, estimates from the printer you chose so that you can refer to them often.

The primary advantage of offset printing is its ability to produce photographs and illustrations. You will also be able to have your book done in any trim size and bound as you wish. If you need a special size trim or want a hardcover, this is the best way to go. The disadvantage to this method of printing is that, the larger the print run, the lower the cost per book. Even if you decide to order a relatively small print run of 500 and pay the extra cost, you still have to have a minimum number of books printed. This forces you to find storage space for all those boxes of books. This drawback has led to the birth of a whole new type of printing process that seems geared for self-publishers.

On-Demand Printing

The print-on-demand, or POD, is a fairly new concept, and a great one for self-publishers. You do not have to order thousands or even hundreds of books and then have to find storage space. You can have as few as one book done at a time. The production cost is usually the same for each book. This can make it easier for you to handle orders. All you need to do is order the number you expect will sell in the near future rather than trying to guess what your whole future market might be. And most POD printers can give a fairly quick turn around time for reprints. It sounds like a perfect solution.

The POD method of printing actually uses a very high-end computerized photocopier. Besides the ability to print only the number of books you need, another advantage is that most of them are set up to have your typeset book put into the machine on a computer disk. This means you do not have to have a camera ready copy made. Although you should provide a hard copy for the printer to refer to, the machine can make your book straight from a disk or e-mailed file. POD printers are not yet set up to make a book from a CD, so do not save to that medium.

The main drawback to this type of printing are the printers themselves. Anyone who can afford to lease one of these machines can call themselves a POD printer. The internet is full of websites touting their services. But do they really know anything about the publishing process? Like all other aspects of business, do your research. Make sure you get not only price quotes, but references from other clients who have had books published. Take a look at other books the printer has done. Do they meet your expectation of a professional looking product? Too many new self-publishers are paying out too much money for an inferior product. It is not that most POD printers are deliberately taking advantage, they often do not know better themselves.

Another drawback to using POD printers is

the type of cover they can provide. Most of them cannot do hard covers while others limit the size of the book due to the inefficiency of their binding machines. Many successful book packagers limit the number of pages of your book because they can only produce a book up to a certain page size. This severely restricts their service to you. You then have to either change the size of your book, change the font and leading, or change the number of pages with a serious rewrite. If your book is fairly small, POD printing is optimum. If it you want it to have a hard cover or wish to keep the length, go to an offset printer.

POD printers are good for small print runs and small books. They are also good for reprints of out-of-print books. They work well for family histories or books put together by an organization to raise money for its cause. They fill a need in the self-publishing world. What you have to do is determine if they fill your need too.

E-BOOKS

You may decide to make your work available online as an e-book. This means you will not have to worry about printers or binders. There would be no paper to buy nor covers to have printed. Your book would be available in either the format of the popular readers such as PalmPilot, in a word processing format, or as a *portable document format* (pdf) file. All of these are set up to be downloaded into the customer's computer after they have given the publisher a credit card number. Some see it as the way of the future and others think it is a passing fad. The truth is that there is an audience for this kind of book but, at the same time, the demand for printed books is larger than ever. Do not try to figure it out. Simply do what is best for you.

Your manuscript must be on a disk or CD in order to make it available online. It must be formatted on the disk. If you decide to go this route, you will need to either have encryption software that ensures the safety of people's privacy when they enter their credit card number, or you will have to use one of the websites who do this for small businesses. Another option is to place your book in several online bookstores made specifically for e-books. For a discount, they will collect payment for your book.

If you wish, you can have both e-books and print copies made to cover both virtual and real bookstores. You might want to consider this as part of your marketing plan. Start out by offering an e-book and, if the market interest is high, have print copies made. Or launch both simultaneously. Just make sure your marketing plan allows for this. Another option, which you will hear about, is to make your book available as a CD. This is viable only if you are sure your potential readers prefer this format or that your material fits a very small niche. Keep in mind that with all our technological advances, most readers still prefer to curl up with a good made-of-paper volume.

BINDING

If you decide to print your book, it must be put together and covered. This is called *binding*. Books can be covered in paper, cloth, or leather. Paper is the most commonly used medium today because cloth and leather are fairly expensive. These latter two often come with a book jacket to protect them. Do not mistake a softcover book for a mass published paperback. The former is like the book you are reading and the latter is a pocket novel. Take a look at any of these you have around the house and you can see the difference in quality.

The binding process involves putting together the galleys of your book. Depending on what printing company you have decided on, your pages could either be printed out in a stack or on large press sheets. With a stack, the book is bound and then cut to size. Larger sheets first have to be folded and collated, and then bound. They must be sized before binding. Many older books about self-publishing go into detail about this process. It is not necessary for you to be concerned about the *signatures* unless your offset printer brings to your attention that you have an odd number of pages. By this I mean that your book length is not divisible by 32, 16, or 8. In which case, you end up paying for unused pages. POD printers do not use signatures.

A large question many first time self-publisher's have is whether to laminate their soft covers. The answer is an unequivocal "yes". Many POD printers will recommend against it since they claim humidity can make the covers curl. This tells you they are not using a very good quality laminating material. Professional binders use a laminating material that does not curl. What it does do is protect the cover of your book. You cannot sell books that have acquired scuff marks from rubbing against other books in the box. Laminated covers will protect against scuffing and keep their appearance well.

THEN WHAT?

After your books are printed, you need to check them out. An average size paper box will hold 80-90 books. Open your boxes up and randomly select books. Look at the cover to make sure there is no damage or scuff marks. Set aside all damaged books and return them to the printer or binder. Take the rest home and get ready to set your marketing plan in motion.

Your books should be printed at least three months before your release date. Too often self-publishers get their books a week or two (or less) before the release date. Publishers do not work with such a short turn around time because they know they need copies on hand to send out. Their distributors will need to have the books before the release date too. Pre-release copies also need to be sent to reviewers. You will learn more about how to get reviews in a later chapter. For now, enjoy the fact that you are an author. You have written and published a book – a feat which many dream of and few ever realize. Now the hard work begins.

CHAPTER 5
Minding Your Self-Publishing Business

The single most valuable skill in business...
is the ability to make the right decisions
most of the time.
– Charles Templeton
Media Personality

HOME BASED BUSINESS

For many of you, this will be the first time you have ever run your own business. While the business of self-publishing will probably not make you rich, it is still a business with all the ensuing decisions and problems that come along with it. You have to get a business number, pay taxes, and keep books. You might make a profit, and you might not. Few people are highly successful in self-publishing. Of course, you may not be in this for money at all. In order to at least recover your investment, you need to pay close attention to managing your self-publishing business.

Some of you will have already experienced the joys of self employment. You may have a wealth of knowledge about running a small or home-based business. You will also understand some of the pitfalls awaiting you. And you know from first-hand experience the thrill of making your own decisions. For those of you who have never tried self-employment, this chapter suggests some ideas to help you out. In addition, you can easily find business books in libraries, bookstores, and financial institutions. Federal and provincial governments, as well as banks, give them away for free. To be honest, it is possible to end up with a fairly large library of how-to and where-to-find books so try not to go overboard.

NAME

Every business needs a distinctive name. Write out several that you like. Then go to the library and look up PUBLISHERS in *RR Bowker's Books in Print*. See if the name you want is already taken. Under certain circumstances, you may use an untrademarked business name that is being used by someone in another province or country, but that is not advisable. If the other business has a bad reputation, you will get to share that too. It is best to come up with an original name for your business.

Many self-publishing experts recommend that you not use your own name as in *John Doe Publishing*. If you do, it will be a dead giveaway that you are an author-publisher. Even though this might sound deceitful, it is done because you do not always benefit from being known as a self-publisher. At the same time, many large publishing companies are made up of the owners' surnames, such as McClelland & Stewart Inc., and it comes across as sophisticated. Paradoxically, along the way you cannot completely hide the fact you are an independent publisher. Cute names can either well work for you or very much against you. Give the name great thought. It is your choice how you wish to proceed. In this case, at this stage you will probably have only one book on your list. Some distributors and bookstores will not even deal with a publisher that does not have a decent sized book list. But do not be deterred. At the very least, you will have local sales and tax deductions.

In some Canadian provinces you do not have to register the name of your business if you actually do business under your own name such as *John Doe Publishing*. You are only required to register the name if you use a trade name (ie: *Half Acre Publishing*), or have another person or persons in the name as in *John Doe and Sons*. In other provinces you are required to have all business names searched for a fee, and then register the business name for another fee. Fees vary across the country. To find out if you have to register a business name in your province, contact your provincial Business Service Centre listed in the appendix. Or check the Canadian Business Service Centre website at *www.cbsc.org* and click on the flag for the province or territory you reside in.

Now you have to decide if you want your self-publishing business to be a *proprietorship* or a *partnership*. A proprietorship is a business that is owned and operated by one person. A partnership is a business that one or more other people also own and operate with you. Be very sure of the person or persons you are going into business with if you are forming a partnership. Both types of small businesses are tied into your personal income. A third option is to *incorporate*. Unless your business grows substantially, it is not the best way to proceed because it can cost a lot of money. However, the major advantage to incorporating is that the business is responsible for any debts incurred, rather than you personally. Unfortunately, at this time, many large companies want personal guarantees. A good accountant can give you sound advice on the tax strategies that will work best for you and your business.

BUSINESS NUMBER

In January 1995, Revenue Canada introduced a new business identification system. The

Business Number (BN) system replaces all the numbers once required to conduct business in Canada. It includes the GST/HST, payroll deductions, corporate income tax, and import/export accounts. The federal government is trying to simplify the process of starting a business.

To receive a BN you have two options. If there is no Canada Customs and Revenue Agency office in your community, call the toll free number of the one nearest you. The people are very helpful and patient with beginners. If you do have a CCRA office in your community, you can drop in and use the new Business Registration On-line (BRO) workstations. These self-help computers are located in the offices and easy to use. You should be able to complete your registration in about 15 minutes. Either way, make sure you have your social insurance number, the business mailing address, and date of your fiscal year-end handy when registering your new publishing business.

GST/HST

Since its inception, we have all learned to live with the Goods and Services Tax. Nova Scotia, New Brunswick, Newfoundland and Labrador have decided to implement the HST or Harmonized Sales Tax which blends their GST and PST into one tax. And, to the deep sorrow of many, most books sold in Canada are taxable. No province at this time is charging Provincial Sales Tax on books, but they are subject to federal tax.

If your business grosses more than $30,000 per year, you have to collect GST for the government, and you have to remit their share. Probably the only CCRA account you will have is a GST/HST one. You collect 7% on each book, hang on to it until you get your statement, and then you send it in. Pretty simple actually. If you live in an HST province, you are not required to collect more than the GST portion of 7%. If you are unsure how to proceed, obtain the GST/HST information guide from CCRA or ask your accountant.

You do not have to register for GST/HST if your business's gross taxable revenue is less than $30,000 per year. If you do not register, you can use all the GST that you pay as an allowable expense rather than become a GST collector. This can be a large tax advantage for you depending on your personal income.

You are allowed to register, and there are two ways to proceed. If you do register, then everything you have paid GST/HST on is refunded to you. Consider the cost of printing. For every $1000 you spend, you will pay $70 in GST or more in HST. Wouldn't it be nice to get that back? You will have paid for typesetting services, bought stationary supplies, paid for book production, and a myriad of other business necessities. You might as well get some of the money back. And if your book sells well, then you already have the account in place. You collect the GST/HST like you would for any business. The difference is when you make your remittance. If you paid out more GST/HST than you collected, the government lets you keep that and will even send you a cheque for the difference. It is important to discuss GST/HST options with your accountant.

When you register you will be asked if you want to remit annually or quarterly. It is tempting to do the paperwork once a year only. But remitting quarterly has its advantages. First, if CCRA owes you money, you get it sooner. This can be very helpful in the early days of your business when you need maximize cash flow. For example, if your book is released in the spring, you will not receive any money until the following year. Second, if you owe CCRA, you do not have to keep the money for very long. Surprisingly, this can be a problem for many and unpaid portions can result in legal action by the federal government. Do your bookkeeping carefully to make sure you do not spend CCRA's portion. Better to pay them quarterly and be done with it.

People are often intimidated by government paperwork. The GST/HST remittance form is very easy to complete. It is a fill-in-the-blanks form with instructions on each line. It is only a

single page long with a working section at the
top, and a detachable section you send in. All
pertinent business information is preprinted on
the form. They even throw in an envelope. Do not
be afraid of GST/HST. It is simply a part of doing
business.

BANK ACCOUNT

After you have a name and BN, you need to
open a business account at a financial institution. Each bank and credit union has its own pro-
cedures. Most, though, have a business department. Make an appointment to see someone to
help you set up the kind of account you will need.
Carefully explain the kind of business you will be
running so you can get the best advice.

Some business bank representatives will give
you booklets and information on being in business
for yourself. Some might even want you to write a
business plan. You have to decide what is right for
your self-publishing business. If you are only going
to have a short printing of a local history and never
plan to write another book, you do not really need
to write a business plan. On the other hand if you
think you are going to self-publish books for many
years, it might not hurt to put one together. Discuss
this with your bank representative.

Your business account at a financial institution it will need to be a chequing account. This is
the best way to keep track of money deposited

and spent. It will help your accountant figure out profits and losses at tax time. You should receive a statement once a month which allows you to reconcile the account. This is done just like you do with your personal chequing account, assuming you reconcile your personal account. Today, financial institutions offer bank cards that you can use to make deposits or withdrawals. The convenience of being able to make deposits anytime is very valid. I recommend that you make it a practice to withdraw funds only by cheque. That is still the best way to keep a paper trail.

BOOKKEEPING

Some of you might enjoy the prospect of keeping a set of books. Others of you will have an anxiety attack. There seems to be no middle ground on the subject. But businesses must keep accurate records, and bookkeeping is one of the necessary evils that come with the deal. If the books are set up properly during the start up of a business, and kept up, they should not pose a problem. There is also the question of whether to do the books manually or on the computer. This is a personal decision. If you do not feel comfortable with a computer, you should do your record keeping manually. Launching a small business is not the time to learn how to use new software. When I published my first book, I did not think the sales volume on a single product justified using a computer bookkeeping program. I used a standard ledger and file folders for all my receipts. Do what ever feels most comfortable for you.

If you have no experience with bookkeeping, and maybe have problems keeping your personal accounts in order, you should probably find someone to help you. It is not necessary to hire a service (unless you want to). You can have a partner, family member, or friend help you set up and maintain the books. The important thing is to keep the books up to date. An accountant once told me if I brought my year end books into his office in a plastic garbage bag, he would charge me accordingly. In other words, the cost of having an accounting firm clean up your bookkeeping mess is pretty high. A little housekeeping on your part will keep that from happening to you.

Putting your books together and taking them to an accountant is important for filing your income taxes. Accountants know how the tax system works and keep up to date on tax regulations. There is a fee for having an accountant do your year end paperwork, but it is tax deductible. Consider that you will probably receive a larger refund by having a professional take care of the year end stuff and you will see it is worth the cost. Whether you use the services of a Chartered Accountant or a Certified General Accountant is strictly up to you.

CREDIT CARDS

When you are in a business that sells a retail product, some customers will want to make purchases with their credit card. Depending on how you market your book, you may or may not need to offer that service. The first thing to know is that it costs money to offer sales by credit card. The second, and very important, thing to know is that you have to put up a fairly large deposit if you plan to have credit card sales via mail order or over the Internet. The reason is that you do not actually see the credit card and are more susceptible to fraud.

You do not need to offer credit card sales if you expect to market your books through a distributor or wholesaler, since you will not be selling directly to the consumer. If you even sell just to local bookstores you will not need that either because bookstores are invoiced. It is when you sell directly to customers that they will ask if they can pay with a card. I recommend you talk this over with your accountant and bank representative before making the decision. Fortunately, it is not one you have to make when you are just starting out.

Managing your self-publishing business will be an adventure. It can either be an exciting adventure or a frustrating one, depending on how well you keep on top of the business details. If you are unsure of this part of self-publishing, get someone to help you. Do not let the task of bookkeeping take away the joy of producing a book in print. Remember that you will be wearing many hats. And one of them has to be the businessperson's hat.

CHAPTER SIX
Before the Release Date

*Doing business without advertising is like
winking at a pretty girl in the dark
– you know what you're doing, but nobody
else does.*
— Murray Koffler
Pharmacist and Philanthropist

PREPUBLICATION

A book is not considered to be actually published until it is finally released for the public to purchase and read. Until then, you have even more work to do in order to give your book the best chance in the marketplace. By now, you should have started your own publishing business, and have a completely formatted book which should be either at the printer or ready to go. You should have decided on cost, page count, and the date of publication (or release). If you have planned properly, you will be well within your schedule. Now the real work begins.

In the trade publishing industry, books can take as much as a year or two from the time the manuscript is accepted until it is made available to the public in bookstores and libraries. During the process of making a book, the editor is busy preparing the press and bookstores for release of the book. Giving out this information usually takes place about six months before the release date. I do not recommend you put it off for any less than three or four months, or you may not be viewed kindly by either reviewers or distributors. One of the main reasons these people do not like to accept self-published material is because it is not usually offered in either a professional manner or time frame. Prepublicity must be factored into your schedule.

Prepublication is a very important step to self publishing. If you do it well, it may be what sells your book. If you do it badly, you may end up regretting that you ever tried to publish a book yourself. If you are shy about "tooting your own horn" you might need help at this step. Publicists and publicity firms come in all price ranges. On the other hand, your skills as a writer will serve you well at this stage. You can send out packages to reviewers, register with all the industry databases, and write news releases and advertisements. Your business self and your writing self blend at this point.

MARKETING PLAN

Most endeavours in this world are more successful when a plan is in place. You need a marketing plan in order to have a step-by-step "map" to guide you through the process of selling your book. The easiest way to start is by brainstorming ideas and writing them down. Get friends and family involved in this kind of session. After you complete the list, you can start to look at what you are prepared to do to sell books.

Begin by deciding the level of marketing you plan to do – national, regional, or local. Make a list of the print media and broadcast media you want to send press packages to. Put together a list of people who you would like testimonials from. Then write a letter of request for testimonials from each one of them. The next list to write is of any newsletters, printed or online, that you think might be interested in your book. These tend to be topical and have a dedicated readership. Then list the booksellers you plan to approach, along with their contact information. What a lot of lists to make! And you could use more – lists of where you want to have book signings, lists of catalogues that might carry your book, lists of media where you might want to place paid ads, and on and on. Be creative, and you might surprise yourself at how many venues you come up with to publicize your book. The next chapter will cover marketing and you may want to add those ideas to your lists.

Part of your marketing plan should include writing a first draft of your news release and any articles you think might appeal to print media on your lists. You can write final drafts later. If you can come up with more than one angle for your material, write more than one article. Make a list of website designers. Decide what you want to put on your website. Make a list of keywords and reciprocal links for your website, and set up a press room on your website.

As you can see, devising a marketing plan requires a lot of creative thinking. Actually, it is mostly thinking and writing ideas down on lists. From these, you will "fill in the blanks" with names and contact information. Each time you read about something or come up with another idea, write it down. I keep a file folder handy to put all the lists and notes into as they accumulate. I label it "Marketing" and that way I will not lose any ideas or information that I have. Your marketing plan and file containing information will help you to stay organized. When things start to take off, you will appreciate feeling like you are organized somewhere.

LISTS AND DATABASES

Before your book goes to print, you will need to order the CIP information to put on the legal page. This was discussed in Chapter 3. By taking part in the CIP program, your book will automatically be put into their catalogue and database. You also want to register with the Canadian Books in Print program. Your book will also be listed in *Quill and Quire Fall Announcements,* an annual supplement to the magazine. This will increase your exposure. None of this costs more than the price of a postage stamp and envelope, so make sure you take advantage of it. After that, you will receive a copy of a printout about your book each year in May. You can make corrections if necessary. Send it back by early June, and your book stays current in the database.

Another important database I have already discussed is R.R. Bowker's *Books in Print* and new *Global Books in Print.* This is a huge database that will put your book into their electronic catalogue. They offer information about millions of books to libraries and bookstores. They are obviously interested in listing self-published books, as there is an article on the subject on their website. It is worth viewing at ***www.bowker.com***. To submit a book to their database, use their new BowkerLink. It is a very simple step-by-step online form.

REVIEWS

Most of us have read book reviews in various newspapers. Many of the large dailies will do reviews, but smaller community papers also write them and can result in a full page article with photos. Community papers will tie their story in to you as a local author. Regional papers might also be willing to give you coverage because you are a provincial or regional author.

Reviews can be beneficial for your book sales. I cannot overemphasize their importance . In fact, the best thing you can do for your book is to get great reviews. As a self publisher, the luckiest thing you can do is get any reviews. You may be told that reviewers will not look at self published books. Truthfully, this is often the case. You are competing with established publishers who know most of the reviewers and produce a good product. It is not easy to have your book reviewed, so you have to carefully target the publications you want to send a review package out to.

Most reviews come from newspapers or a magazines. If you get a good review, you can have it printed on your book cover. You can excerpt a review and use only the part you need. Remember, though, to keep the spirit of what the reviewer had written or you will risk losing your credibility. You will need to make copies of all reviews and articles to include in your media package. Every time you receive a review, update your media package.

The most obvious place to start is Canada's large national papers, such as *The Globe and Mail* and *The National Post*. If you think you have a book with national appeal, and can pitch it well, then send a book, or galley, and media package to the book review editor. You can find this information on their websites. Most of us do not have books with national appeal and we need to look closer to home for our reviews. The next place to look is your large regional or provincial daily newspaper. They might decide to review your book because you are a local author. Use this hook when you are preparing your media list. If they decide to profile you or your book, you might have to travel to the city where the newspaper is produced for a photo. If that is not possible, ensure you include a photo of yourself holding your book in your media package. We will discuss in detail what to put into a media package later in this chapter.

Many Canadian communities have small community newspapers that get delivered for no charge because the advertising covers the costs. Here is probably one of your best opportunities to get a review. Often you can get a half or full page write up along with a photo. You would be amazed at how widely newspapers of this type are distributed. If they had a subscription list, it would be quite large.

Magazines do not necessarily review books *per se*, but they do write articles about books. Authors often include their opinions about the material at the same time. A public library is the best place to find magazines that you would like to send your book, or galley, and media package to. You can look at current and back issues to determine if your subject matter is appropriate to that publication. Another place to look is *The Canadian Writer's Market,* which you should be able to find in any bookstore. Canadian magazines are listed, along with information on the kind of material they publish. If you can imagine your book's subject in there, put them on your list. If you think your book has a larger appeal, have a look at *Writer's Digest Writer's Market* to find American magazines you can contact. Always think about who would be interested in the subject of your book and how an article about your book might be received. Be prepared to write your own article, if necessary, to get the publicity.

Another source of reviews could be a person, sometimes an expert in the field or someone who is well known or whose opinion others respect. Start by looking for someone that you know and who would be willing to read the manuscript or galley, and give you their opinion. If they like the book and you like their opinion, ask them to write a review. Do not be surprised if you are expected to pay, though. Experts and well known people are asked so frequently to do things like this, they simply cannot do it for free. Of course, if the expert or famous person happens to be a member of the family or a close friend, this should not come up.

Does paying negate the review? The answer is no. Reviewers for newspapers and writers for magazines are paid for what they do. As long as you are clear up front that the reviewer can say what they believe, do not worry about paying them. This is not the same as offering to pay someone to write a great review. Experts and well known people care about their reputation and can usually be counted on to give you an honest appraisal. And if you do not like the review, do not use it.

A surprising part of the book publishing process is that you often have to write the review yourself. Again, well known people are usually very busy. What they want from you is a review that they can edit. It sounds odd, but that is the way personal reviews are done. Writing your own review will be one of the hardest things for you to do. You have to say something dynamic about your book and try to keep in mind what your intended reviewer might say. Thinking in the third person takes some practice. While you might actually feel comfortable writing in the third person, it will seem strange to be writing about yourself and your book.

INFORMATION SHEETS

Just about everything you send out must include an information sheet about your book. Whether you submit material to the media or a

catalogue, you need to provide certain information about your book. An information sheet should include the following:
> title
> author
> publication date
> ISBN
> publisher name and contact information
> price
> number of pages and trim size
> number of illustrations
> distributor contact (if being carried by one)

Some information sheets will require a short write up, or blurb, about the book. I recommend you write three of them – 30 words, 50 words, and 85 words. Keep them all handy because you will find that you are often required to tell about your book in a few words. For this book I built my blurbs one on the other. They all have the same beginning sentences, and I kept adding to each blurb until I got to my word count. It is also a great writing exercise.

Many sources for information sheets tell you to include the name and contact information for the publicist. In this case that person is you! If you want to put on that hat on, so to speak, go ahead. Just remember, your name is the same as the author's. Of course this gives away the fact that the book is self-published. At the same time, if you act professionally and do not look silly, you will have a better chance of being noticed.

INFORMATION SHEET

Self Publishing in Canada: A complete guide to designing, printing and selling your book
By Suzanne Anderson
Release October 2003
1-894208-00-5
Reference/Writing
Foreword by Dan Poynter
Non-Fiction
Softcover / 5.5" x 8.5" / 288 pages / 7 illustrations
$24.95 (Cdn) plus shipping
Returns must be made within one year in new condition, prepackaged and prepaid.

Half Acre Publishing
7311 Bell McKinnon Road
Duncan BC V9L 6A8
PH/FAX: 250-746-3919
halfacre@selfpublishing.ca
www.selfpublishing.ca

Figure 4

MEDIA PACKAGES

When you approach the media, whether it be print, radio or television, you need to provide a media, or press, package in a presentation folder with your business card attached either on the inside or outside. If you choose to place your business card in the spot inside where the folder is cut for them, also make a label for the outside of the cover. Members of the media can get swamped with these packages. Sometimes they resemble business folders with other material in them and you want to make sure there is no doubt what is inside your folder. Everyone's desk gets covered at some time or another. Make the effort to ensure your press release does not get lost in the mess.

What goes into your media package? Every book you read on the subject and every website you visit will have different information. It can be confusing to a novice. Following is a list that will satisfy the needs of any member of the media and will show that you know what you are doing:

- An information sheet. If you had covers printed on plain paper, you can print the information on the reverse side of them. Do this if you are not sending a book or galley at this time.

- A letter clearly explaining why your book subject is important enough to be reviewed. Use a clear and active voice. This is your *pitch letter*, similar to that of a freelance writer trying to pitch an article to a magazine. Spend a lot of time writing, since it could be your only foot in the door.

- A news release, which I will describe later in this chapter.

- An author's bio and photo. This is an opportunity to give details about yourself and establish both why you were the best person to write this book and what credentials you have. The photo should be no smaller than 5" x 7" and it does not matter if it is colour or black and white. Try to have a picture taken of you holding your book. If you have a digital camera and a computer, you can print your own public relations photos.

- A bookmark or post card, which we will discuss in the chapter on marketing. You can use the post card for requesting acknowledgement that the media package arrived safely. Print "I have received the media package from (your publishing company)" on the back. Do not forget to print your mailing address on it and affix a postage stamp.

- A page of testimonials if you have some by now. This shows a reviewer that others have read and appreciated your book. Make sure you write the quotes in italics and the name in regular font. If you are not submitting your information sheet on the extra covers of your book, print the testimonials on them instead.

Any time you receive a review, photocopy it and include it in all your media packages. Shrink a long review down to fit on either letter or legal size paper. Staple copies together if the review is on more than one page. Oddly enough, reviewers are more interested if others have reviewed your book. It tells them that your subject must be timely and interesting. It also tells them that someone else has considered your book seriously enough to write about it.

Offer to write an article for other publications if you have that skill. Many times that will be the only way to get publicity for your book. Small print media and busy ones both will look favourably at an offer of an article. It is important, though, that you know how to write in this specialized format. It is very different from writing a book. Word count is important and, like a news release, it has a standard format. While an article is not as structured as a news release, the standard format still has to be followed. Most local colleges offer courses or workshops on article or freelance writing. It might be a worthwhile investment for you to take one.

NEWS RELEASE

A news release, or press release, is a great way to publicize your book. Small newspapers will often run it as is. Larger newspapers might run it as you have written it or use parts of it as filler. Either way, it is free. If you do not know how to write a news release, check on the internet or for books on the subject that even have samples in them. If you really cannot write a news release, find someone else to do it for you. This is one time it is worthwhile to pay someone to write for you.

Your release should be on 8-1/2" x 11" paper and kept to one page in length. Your headline needs to grab the reader's attention. Figure out a "hook" and keep to that theme. Remember to use the five "W's" in your first paragraph - *who, what, where, when, why*, and sometimes *how*. Each succeeding paragraph should be of declining importance in case the press release needs to be shortened. You do not want to have important information chopped off. Use short words and sentences. This is for a newspaper and they have a specific way they want copy written. If you are still in doubt, have a good look at some newspapers. Check out your nearest big city, your own town, and the national papers. The illustration on this page is a sample of a news release.

How do you get a news release out to the media? If it is not in a press package, either e-mail or FAX it. Although the technology is in place, many media outlets still do not take press releases by e-mail. Even the smallest of papers receive releases and CP information via the FAX machine. If the media you are sending your news release to does accept e-mailed submissions, do

FOR IMMEDIATE RELEASE

Contact: Suzanne Anderson
           Half Acre Publishing
           Phone/FAX: 250-746-3919
           halfacre@selfpublishing.ca
           www.selfpublishing.ca

SELF-PUBISHING IN CANADA MADE EASIER

(Duncan, BC, October 30, 2003) – As self-publishing fast becomes a real option in Canada, a source of current information for both the beginner and the more experience author has appeared on the horizon. Half Acre Publishing announced today the publication of a new book entitled SELF PUBLISHING IN CANADA – A COMPLETE GUIDE TO DESIGNING, PRINTING AND SELLING YOUR BOOK, by Suzanne Anderson. Delivering accurate book design standards and current internet resources, this book will help the self-publisher compete for shelf space in bookstores.

Self-publishing is no longer the last resort of a desperate writer. It is a valid option given today's technology and it is rapidly gaining popularity in Canada. With the demise of General Distribution Services, and the ensuing fallout, more and more writers are turning to the independent method of publishing in order to get their books in the hands of the reading public. Now there is a book that will unlock the secrets to self-publishing in Canada.

Anderson is an experienced self-published author. She has worked as a freelance writer and is currently on the board of directors for a self-publishing co-operative on Vancouver Island. She conducts workshops on both self-publishing and book marketing at various colleges. Her website is www.selfpublishing.ca.

-30-

Figure 5 - Sample News Release

not send the press release as an attachment. Most media do not open attachments. Cut, or copy, and paste the release into the body of the email.

ADVERTISING

Surprisingly, many people are not quite sure what the difference is between *publicity* and *advertising*. Publicity usually comes free of charge and advertising normally requires payment. Publicity is a news release or article in the local paper, while advertising is a paid advertisement in the same paper. You want to try to gather as much publicity as possible, but sometimes it is worthwhile to pay for an ad.

When you decide to advertise, you really have to put on a business hat. The cost of ads can be very high and you want to spend no more than 5% of your total marketing budget on paid ads. You need to be creative to make the most of your advertising budget. A catch phrase today is to "think outside the box". Either devise an ad that gets your message across effectively, or target specific media where you will be placing the ad. We all know the world of advertising is complex, and we are mostly amateur. So how do you know where to spend your money?

A half page ad in *The Globe and Mail* will cost over $3500. You certainly would not spend that much on an ad in your local or regional newspaper. Perhaps you cannot afford the rate for an ad in *The Globe and Mail*, but you should be able to afford to be included in *The Independent Publishers' Bookshelf*. This is a twice yearly supplement put out by *The Globe and Mail* for independent (or self) publishers like ourselves and the cost is only $325 per title. As we normally do not have more than one title, this is a good deal.

Canada's largest circulation newspaper about books is *BC Bookworld*. This western Canadian quarterly has 100,000 readers who include members of the industry and the general reading public. While anyone can subscribe and have it delivered, issues are free in many bookstores. A sixteenth page vertical ad costs $200.00 for one issue. That actually only works out to fractions of a penny per reader and is a good buy.

Catalogues are another good place to advertise. It can usually cost much less than $100 to buy space in a book catalogue. Find out where the catalogue is being distributed and how many will be printed. Do not be surprised at the variance either. Catalogues run from 500 copies to 500,000. You will have to provide a list of information similar to the information sheet I have already discussed. You will also need to have a digital picture of the cover of your book. Actually, this is a good thing to have saved on a disk because you never know when the need will pop up. Make sure it is no larger than 100 dpi and saved in a .jpg format. While some catalogues will take .gif or .tif files, pretty well everyone wants a JPEG.

Radio is a medium that new author-publishers seldom think of. If your book has a wide audience you might consider Radio-TV Interview Report at **www.rtir.com**, which is a U.S. based directory of new books and is delivered to American TV and radio producers every couple of weeks. The cost is less than $300 (US) and can result in interviews.

Marketing professionals say the best place to spend your advertising dollar is by advertising not directly to the consumer, but in trade magazines that are read by librarians and booksellers. Their opinions are respected and, best of all, they make recommendations to their customers. In Canada we have *Quill & Quire* at **www.quillandquire.com** and *Canadian Bookseller* at **www.cbabook.org**.

However, there is no guarantee you will increase book sales by advertising. You could spend good money and not receive a single extra order from it. That is why you need to put your business hat firmly on your head and make some serious decisions. Well placed and well planned ads can increase your chances of increasing book sales. But you may decide there is no need to advertise. Remember, most books still sell best by word-of-mouth. All the advertising dollars in the world cannot change that single fact. It is your call.

All this work needs to be done before you actually release your book. That means you have a lot of pre-planning to do. This aspect of self-publishing is very much on the business side. Those who love to write and hate to do business often do not like this aspect of self-publishing. Others find it challenging to come up with creative ways to sell books. Even if you do not like to do your own marketing, remember that books do not sell themselves and you really have to plan for getting your book out. If it is too uncomfortable for you, get help from a spouse, friend, or even a professional. Do not neglect this aspect of self-publishing. It is far too important.

CHAPTER SEVEN
Books for Sale!

Radio is a 'hot' medium and is
indispensable when the issues get hot.
TV is a fantasy medium, and has good
reason to be called 'cool'.
— Marshall McLuhan
Communications Theorist

MARKETING

Marketing is the most important step in the publishing process. If you do not market your books, they will not sell. In fact, they will end up sitting in boxes in your garage or basement taking up floor space. This crucial step is very definitely part of the business of self-publishing. You have to start to think of your books as products now — and a product to be moved out quickly. This phase of self-publishing is where the real work begins.

There are almost as many ways to sell books as there are books to be sold. You should already have your marketing plan made and be ready to activate it. This is the time to go over the plan to select which ideas you like from those you do not. Decide which ideas you think are feasible and decide which ones will work for your book. Now, finalize your list and start telling the world that you have books for sale.

WORD OF MOUTH

Believe it or not, the best marketing tool is word of mouth. When people read a book and like it, they tell their friends, who also read it and tell their friends. Many bestsellers have emerged as a result of this simple principle. One example is *The Christmas Box* by Richard Paul Evans. He wrote the story in 1994 for his daughters and printed a few copies for them and their friends. Every week he received requests for more books. He did not advertise, but every week he was printing more and more books. Finally, a large publisher made him a nice offer to publish the book. It has sold millions of copies around the world, proving how powerful word of mouth can be.

DIRECT MAIL

A popular way for author/publishers to sell their products is by direct mail where readers send you their order along with a cheque or money order, and you mail the books out. This is a simple way to sell books. You do not have to deal with anyone in the middle such as a distributor or bookstore. If you are uncomfortable selling in person, this may be the best route for you. You gather orders that come in the mail and send out books. Just make sure you factor the cost of postage and envelopes into the total cost. These are business expenses and can be tax deductible. One advantage to selling this way is that you can charge less for the book since you will not have to look at discounts. Your books will sell for the price you set.

Certain types of books lend themselves more readily to mail order, usually non-fiction and how-to books. If you have done your research, you will have a clear idea of whether your book is right for mail order. If your market is made of people who would normally order by mail, you may do quite well. There are many good books about how to be successful with mail order sales. Invest in a few and educate yourself. People with a good product to sell have become financially successful this way.

The best place to advertise your mail order book for sale is on a website. I will discuss that later in this chapter. You can also advertise in the classified sections of newspapers and magazines. Large newspapers will be more expensive than local ones, so decide where to find your market. Many specialty magazines have a classified section in the back. Surprisingly these can be a significant place to gather orders.

Write a small intriguing ad. Keep it brief because you pay by the word. Do not ask for a SASE since you are expected to pay for shipping, but make sure the cost is figured into your total price. You should not run the ad less than three issues since that is how long it normally takes to impress people. To "key" ads, make minor changes to your address such as adding an "a" after the house number in the address. What this does is give you a clear picture where your books are selling. It can also be used to test various ads to see which draw the best response. Based on what you learn from keying your ad, make changes.

One proven method of successful mail order is to send order forms out to prospective customers. I do not recommend you use the addresses everyone you have ever been associated with or are related to. Rather, purchase a mailing list to target your audience. They are not very expensive and are readily available on the internet. Decide who your potential readers are by either interest or demography, and contact a company that sells lists. You can either receive pre-printed labels or a computer file set up so you print the labels yourself. Check with the company you choose to see what their accuracy rate is. You do not want to spend money on a mail out campaign, only to have a large portion returned because the addresses are out of date. Treat it as a business transaction and you could be very successful. Like all other aspects of business, not doing your homework could add unnecessary costs.

ADVERTISEMENTS

To give your book publicity, you could take out paid advertisements in various newspapers and magazines. These are costly and need to be planned well in advance since your ad will compete with those of the trade publishers, who are very proficient advertisers. Most self-publishers do not have the skills to even develop good ads. While the sales person at the publication can help with this, it still needs input from you. Advertising is a profession, and if you are not a professional, you are taking a chance with your investment money. The cost normally runs into the thousands of dollars, so you have to sell a lot of books to make it pay for itself. Many self-publishers believe in generating publicity, which is free, rather than paid advertising. There is merit to that belief.

Globe and Mail has a book section feature called *The Independent Publisher's Bookshelf*. It could be a worthwhile expenditure for a book with primarily a national audience. It would not be useful for a local or regional history or memoir. It can also be a good place for fiction because that tends to cross geographic lines. Since the

Globe and Mail has a large circulation in Ontario, it can be a venue for maritime or western authors to reach that market. So should you do it then? That is a decision only you can make. Look at your expenses and marketing plan. If an ad in this feature is affordable, and if you think you have the right book, then give it a try. If you cannot afford it or your audience is too narrow, do not do it.

There is a group of self-publishers who make a living advertising in the classified sections of magazines. They often have booklets for sale rather than books. Since this is a mail order method, the smaller product keeps the cost of postage down. Some people have been in business for decades selling books and booklets, and have become recognized as experts about their topic. Anything as simple as investment advice to recipes for zucchini will sell. You can often find courses at your local or community college on how to sell this way. It might be worth checking out.

WEBSITES

We are in the information age and websites are nearly as common as books. The internet is a great medium to sell just about anything, including books. It is an easy and inexpensive way to both promote and sell your book. Even if you are not comfortable with a computer, you need to give serious consideration to having your own website. A good site can promote your book, showcase you as an expert, and provide the media with material that you will not have to pay to mail. Your own website lets others know you are abreast of modern marketing techniques.

One big advantage to having your own website is that you can sell e-books. You will need to have your book converted to several formats in order for people to be able to download them. It is recommended that you offer PDF files for Adobe Acrobat, LIT files for MS-Reader with ReaderWorks, and XML/OEB files for regular online reading. Because you do not have many costs involved with this format, you can charge much less for the book. Although there are far more readers of paper books than e-books, the latter are becoming more and more popular.

There are sites on the internet that offer websites to authors, or you can set up your own. The cheapest method to set up your own site is to use the service your internet provider makes available. Most providers give you web space as part of your e-mail plan and usually run from two to five megabytes. You can easily sell one book in this amount of space. The web address would be *YourProvider.com / YourSiteName / AnExtension. html*. This can be a bit long so make sure you use a short, catchy site name. But there is an alternative – you can have your own domain.

My domain is **selfpublishing.ca**. I could not get a .com or even a .net, but the .ca domains had just come out when I decided to get my own domain. More .ca domains are available than the older domain types. You can order a .ca domain either online or from an agent who has permission to register them. Phone any computer shop and ask if they can help. If they cannot, ask them to tell you who can. If you cannot find a source in your community, log on to **www.cira.ca** and find a registrar there. CIRA is the Canadian Internet Registration Authority and they are responsible for registration and monitoring the .ca domains. You will pay a fee for registering as well as a small annual fee when you renew. Because the cost is reasonable, there are even individuals who have their own domain. Do not grab a bunch of domains and sit on them. This is called "squatting" and is frowned upon. On the other hand, grab a domain if it will tie into a future project. That is considered good business sense.

Should you build your own site or have someone else do it? The answer depends a lot on your skills and abilities. If you have to get your nephew or the neighbour's kid to print your work out, then do not even attempt building a website. There are many arguments as to whether you should have a website built professionally or do it yourself. Everyone I talk to tells me it is easy. If you do it yourself you can either learn *html* (hyper text markup language) or you can use software that does it for you. This sounds easy, but really does you little good if you have no concept of good web design. Even a simple one page website requires some sense of design. As a writer you should appreciate that not anyone who can use a computer can write a book. Look at many sites before you decide if you can do it yourself. Some sites will even offer a template for a website and that might be a benefit for you.

If you decide to have someone else build your website, you need to decide who should do it. All of us have family members (usually high school or college students) who may offer to build your site. This is fine if you trust them. Make sure they show you their previous work. Then you need to show them sites you like and let them know what it is that you like about the sites. It may take a fairly long time to have a site built this way since most people really do not comprehend how complex it is to build even a simple site. Sometimes family members or friends cannot seem to grasp your vision. It can lead to frustration or even hard feelings. Like the editing process, do not risk relationships over business issues.

If you decide to either build the site yourself or have a friend/family member do it, you will have to find someone to host your site. You will be charged a set up charge and an annual fee. Unless you are a computer "guru" yourself, you will not understand how to get your site picked up by major search engines. It is no longer a matter of simply having the best *meta tags*.

Research the internet for articles on how to get good positioning with the search engines. Like any marketing medium, you need to ask your business self what you want from a website. If you want a simple, inexpensive site to promote your book, then look at doing it yourself. But when should you hire a professional?

I had family members attempt to build a site for me and it was not working out. I hired a professional web designer. I thought the cost was reasonable since I already knew what I wanted and was going to write all the text myself. The site was up in nine days and exceeded my expectations. All the hosting and editing is done by the webmaster and I can concentrate on what I know best – writing.

Now let us talk about the cost. Many of us go to family members or friends because we think it will cost $2000 or more to have a site built. It can, but it should not be that much. Shop around and get estimates. Look at sites that the company has built and decide if you like their work. One local company I looked at had too many similarities among the sites they had built and I did not like that. Hosting can cost anywhere from $150 per year and up, but $300 per year or more is the norm. Several technical questions need to be answered before you put your site up. A good designer not only knows the questions to ask, but they understand the answers.

On the site, make sure all your pages load

quickly or people will not stop. Do not have too many graphics, banners or flashing icons that are distracting. You can offer book excerpts or whole chapters. In fiction, post the first chapter and let viewers know they can read the rest of the book by ordering it. For non-fiction, consider posting the table of contents or the first page of each chapter. Make it easy for customers to order either by accepting credit cards, setting up an account with an internet payment collection company, or linking to an online bookstore where the book can be purchased. Make sure you can be contacted by both prospective readers and the media. Consider a "press room" at your site with a picture of yourself, the book, an author bio, news releases, story angles, and backgrounders. Also ensure that you provide links to other online sources. But do not just stop there, send a polite email to the webmaster of sites you would like to link to yours. This is called *reciprocal business* and can bring a lot of viewers to your site. Like all other marketing venues, a website should work for you and be within the budget you have planned. It is a business tool so do not let it take over your life.

BOOKSTORES – REAL AND ONLINE

The obvious place to take your books to sell are bookstores. Unfortunately it is not as easy to place your books in them as it once was. Not too many years ago, an independent bookstore would take a few books if you presented yourself professionally. The managers of large chains had small budgets for local books and would talk to you about carrying your book. If you presented terms that were within industry standards, including a return policy, you stood a fair chance of getting your book on a shelf somewhere. Now you pretty much have to either have a distributor or offer the book on consignment. It is time consuming and expensive for a bookstore to set up an account for your little publishing company that has only one book. Actually, many experienced author/publishers will tell you bookstores are the worst places to try to sell books. Consumers purchase more books in specialty stores these days.

You can still try to have a bookstore purchase your book if you feel it is important though. Your presentation has to be professional and meet industry standards. Bookstores receive a minimum 40% discount. Many distributors offer a sliding scale to encourage more sales. Your return policy must be stated clearly. The norm is that you will take the books back in good condition, prepackaged and prepaid, within a year from purchase. The sad reality is that most books are not in good condition when you get them back. You will also find that the definition of good condition is open to interpretation. You are not required to refund the bookstore for books that look like they have been well used. When you sell to bookstores, you have to make sure you have the funds held back to pay them for returns that are in good condition.

Online bookstores do not normally buy books, so you do not have to deal with the hassle of returns. They usually require a setup fee and a percentage of the price of any of your books they sell. They will place your book on their website and customers purchase from them, so you do not have to worry about handling online orders. Amazon.com is the largest and most recognized online bookstore in the world, but there are many other smaller ones. You can also look for resources such as **www.knowbetter.com** that has a database of over 100 online bookstores. Most of them are in the United States and you will be dealing in their currency. When an order is received at the online bookstore, they will inform you and you are usually expected to send the book directly to the customer. Some online bookstores will warehouse a few copies, but do not expect that. Keep your reputation intact by ensuring that you send the books out within two to four days after you receive the order. Research the various sites and requirements carefully. For online bookstores, make sure you have a good quality .jpg digital photo of your book's front cover ready to send to them, along with a short, catchy blurb. This is all the reader will see, and you want to make it stand out.

BOOK SIGNINGS

One of the neatest things about having books carried in a traditional bookstore is the opportunity to have a book signing. Be fore-warned, though, that unless you are famous they are not necessarily well attended and you will probably not sell a lot of books. But it is a great way to generate publicity. Best of all, they cost the author very little except in time and travel. If you live in a large city, you will have several local bookstores to choose from. If you have to travel to various towns and cities, keep track of those costs. Keep receipts and log the mileage for your accountant. Whenever possible, do not have a simple book signing, have an event. By this, I mean offer a mini-workshop or tie it into a theme where people can wear costumes or teach a craft. You can also have a book signing in a specialty store if your topic is relevant. Use your imagination, and it could become an outstanding event.

When you are having a book signing, make sure you confirm the date, time, and address of the bookstore. Take extra copies of your books, a table-cloth that complements your book cover, pens, notepads, tissues, hand lotion, breath mints, and a camera. Make up a name tag so people know you are the author. Bring some things to give away such as bookmarks, photocopied excerpts from the book, a report, and perhaps a dish of candy. Everyone likes a "freebie". You may want to make up labels that say "Signed by author" to place on the cover of any unsold books. Just be sure to actually autograph them. Be pleasant, chatty and witty. Talk to everyone. There are many people who will be shy to approach an author so you have to draw them out. If you are visiting several bookstores in a short time, make up thank you cards in advance for the bookstore owners who host the event. This simple gesture of courtesy will ensure a positive reception if you ever want to come back for another signing.

LIBRARIES

There are approximately 21,000 libraries in Canada. That translates into a lot of readers. If your book has been edited and designed professionally, then you have a good chance of selling to libraries. There are university and college libraries out there as well as public libraries, and because of the geographic nature of our vast country, there are a great many regional library systems. What this means for you is that you need only send literature to one source to cover many libraries. To find addresses of all the libraries, look in *Scott's Canadian Source Book*, which you can find in the reference section of your local library.

One of the nice things about libraries is that they usually pay full price for your book. Mind you, they are grateful for any discount because they are often scrambling for funds, and they often reorder when books become damaged or are stolen. This means repeat business. It is amazing that bookstores will return books when libraries will order more. It shows quite a dramatic difference in how they do business. Selling books to libraries can be lucrative if you have the right book.

You will need to approach libraries the way you approach any bookseller with a well done package. Include an information sheet, making sure this one states what formats are available. Libraries also offer audio cassettes and CDs to their readers. Having had extra covers printed will come in handy now to show what it looks like. It will also show your back cover blurb, which is one of your best selling features. When it comes to stuffing and addressing envelopes, this is a good time to either belong to a co-operative or start one.

Start with your local branches. They often have budgeted for purchasing books by local authors. Offer to put on an event of some kind to attract attention to your book. Libraries never have enough people volunteering to help, so anything you are prepared to do will be greatly appreciated. Not all libraries purchase books directly, so you may have to deal with library services such as John Coutt's Library Services Limited or any other the other large library wholesalers. Your books will come to the attention of libraries when you register on all the lists and databases I discussed in earlier chapters. If your book subject has longevity, contact the library every couple of years to ask if they need to reorder. Getting your books into libraries can be time consuming for you, but it could pay off handsomely in the end.

WHOLESALERS

A wholesaler is a firm that purchases your books at a 50-55% discount and sells them to booksellers. They are set up to warehouse products, fulfill orders, and deliver books. Some specialize in small or independent publishers. I know it can be shocking to be told that the book you have worked so hard at producing, and spent personal money on, is discounted so highly. But that is the cost of doing business. If you have priced your book properly, you can handle the industry discount. The wholesaler has to be paid too, and must give booksellers their customary 40% discount. Some wholesalers will even promote your book along with the other ones they handle. This makes these companies close to being a distributor. You can find a complete list of wholesalers in *Quill & Quire's Canadian Publishers Directory*.

DISTRIBUTORS

Earlier, I said that many booksellers will not buy books from a self-publisher with only one book. They prefer to deal with one source who can provide many books. A wholesaler can fill that role, but the distributor fills that role and more. Distributors actively market your book. They put out catalogues on a regular basis and have representatives in the field. These reps get to know their booksellers and their needs very well. A distributor can open the door to the large chains and retail outlets. This gets into big business and the average author/publisher is not prepared to do business at that level.

For their services, a distributor receives 60-70% of the purchase price of a book. Their discount is higher than that of a wholesaler because they are actively selling your books within the industry. They attend book fairs, conferences, events, and sell outside Canada. They provide a marketing venue and even guidance to the new publisher. If you are serious about large book sales, you almost have to have a distributor to pull it off. Their names are as respected as the trade publishers and that can be a plus when you are trying to sell books.

BOOK CLUBS

Many writers dream of having their books picked up by a book club, a guarantee of sales beyond your imagination. It is not easy to place books in book clubs, but it is possible. You can find a list of book clubs in Canada by going to **www.bookclubdeals.com/canada-book-clubs.html**. From there you can see what the various clubs require. Because you have a single book, they might not deal with you directly, so be prepared to find a wholesaler. Remember to have enough books on hand for a book club – do not print 500 books and expect to have enough. You also have to have a great product, so pay attention to the details of designing your book. When you send a promotion package it has so be some of your best selling to date and will need to include a book rather than cover.

FOREIGN SALES

To us here in Canada, foreign sales also includes the United States. You will need help to find a market and sell to it. You might want to consider an agent for this since you do not likely have the connections that an agent would. Keep in mind that it might be more cost effective to sell print rights than to sell to many foreign countries, and you definitely need an agent to do that. If you are seriously interested in U.S. sales, you will need a distributor. Even though we have a free trade agreement, it is not simple to sell books across the border. There are customs to clear through and the cost could be prohibitive. Leave this to the experts.

OTHER SALES

You might consider finding a catalogue that your book would be appropriate for. Thousands of catalogues are being printed throughout the year, and these sales are not returnable. If you use one yourself, try starting there. Approach the purchaser with a slick package, and see if you can generate interest. You will need to convince the purchaser why your book would be a great product for their customers. Remember, there is a lot of competition out there. There are catalogues for every type of product you can imagine. To find one that might be right for you, look at the *Catalogue of Canadian Catalogues* site at **www.mailordercanada.com**. You will find 1000 catalogues in 130 different categories in their searchable database.

Corporate sales can also be lucrative. If you have a non-fiction book that ties into finance or business practices, you might be able to sell your book to a business or corporation or bank. You might sell a block of non-returnable books to be used either as employee gifts or customer giveaways. If you give seminars based on the material in your book, you might have a product that a corporation would be interested in. When you pitch your book to a corporation, include an autographed copy of the book as well as publicity material with your cover letter. Research the company to target specifically why your book would be worth buying and find the name of the person you should deal with. If you are unsure, try contacting the CEO directly.

Sometimes a book will be suitable to help raise money for your favourite charity. As for catalogues and corporations, you will have to pitch your idea. In this case, though, you donate a portion of sales to the charity rather than sell books outright. An endorsement from the charity can help sell books, because Canadians are supportive of charities. Because Virginia Brucker of British Columbia had lost friends to cancer, she wrote *Gifts From The Heart: 450 Simple Ways to make Your Family's Christmas More Meaningful* to help raise money for the Canadian Cancer Society, who reviewed and endorsed the manuscript before it went to print. The cover informs prospective readers that the purchase of the book helps fund cancer research. Twenty-five percent of the price of each book sold goes to the Cancer Society. Brucker sold the first 2500 copies in six weeks. This can be a true win-win situation for both the self-publisher and the charity.

CHAPTER EIGHT
Getting Them Out

When a thing is current, it creates currency.
– Marshall McLuhan
Communications Theorist

FULFILLING ORDERS

Now that you have publicized and marketed your books, you need to be ready for people to purchase them. Orders have to be filled quickly and professionally. If you do not fulfill orders properly, book sales will dry up. Do not think your work is done now, and that you can now sit back and let the money roll in. You have to send books out to wholesalers, distributors, book-stores, and individual customers.

Most of your mail orders will come from either distributors, wholesalers, or bookstores. When an order arrives, read it carefully. There will be a *purchase order number* on it if it is from a business. You need to quote this on all future correspondence, including invoices. Check that the correct price has been quoted. If you have an ISBN from someone else's list, the orders will go to their place. Check with them frequently so you can get your book or books out in a timely fashion. You should have your books on their way within 2-4 days. Depending on which method you choose to ship, it will take time for the order to reach the customer. If you sit on the order too long, you will have an unhappy customer. You are now in the retail business and must endeavour to keep your customers happy at all cost.

Canada does not have a mailing rate for books. If your book is no larger than 5.5" x 8.5" and no thicker than half an inch, you can put it into an envelope with small bubbles on the inside and it will cost you letter rate. If it is any larger, it will travel as a parcel. In order to help small business, Canada Post has introduced the *VentureOne* card to help save on shipping costs. You receive 5% savings on various types of shipping. Because of this, it is sometimes less expensive to send parcels by the expedited rate rather than regular. You will also receive $100.00 worth of insurance at no extra cost and a tracking number. To find out more about this program, go to your local post office and speak to someone, or check out their website at **www.canadapost.ca**.

You will need to purchase envelopes to mail your books in. In order to protect the book, buy the ones with the bubbles inside. You can find these at any business supply store. If you order 500 or more, you can often get a deal on the order, so shop around. At the same time you will need to purchase shipping labels. I recommend you use 2"x4" for your outgoing label. They are easy to make up on the computer and are large enough for your logo or other graphic you wish to print on it. Use 1"x2" for your return address labels. That will give you enough room to print your website or e-mail address on it too. These can also be purchased at any business supply store. For larger orders, use brown parcel paper and bubble wrap. I usually place a piece of plain paper between the books so they do not rub on each other and risk damaging the covers. If damaged goods are received by the customer, you are responsible for the postage to have them returned. You then have to pay postage to send out more books. The best advice is to do it right the first time.

Set up a specific place to process and fulfill orders. It might be in your basement, your home office, or even on the end of your dining room table. When you receive the order, read it carefully so you will not make a mistake. If there is something you do not understand, contact the customer who made the order. Make a file folder marked *Pending Orders* and keep orders in there until you get to them. Sometimes this will be a purchase order and sometimes it will be a letter or note from an individual. Fill out an invoice, take a book out of a box, and put the two into a envelope. Whether you choose to print the shipping label before or after this step will not make a difference. Affix postage if you are sending by postal rate. If your book is large enough to be a parcel, take it to the post office or a postal outlet to have it weighed and priced. You do not need to rent a postal metre unless you are selling a substantial number of books.

After you process the order, write the date you sent it out on the order form. This way you will have a record of the order in case it either does not arrive or takes an unusually long time to get there. You do not want word to get out that your orders take a long time to be processed. Mark a file folder *Receivables* and move the order into there. When you receive a payment, write the cheque number on both the order form and the invoice, and staple them together. This keeps all documents for each order together. Make a file folder marked *Completed Orders* and put the documents in there. You will keep this until you take it to your accountant at tax time. Afterwards you will archive them. I find that magazine holders make great file folder holders if they are placed long side down. Otherwise, invest in a filing cabinet. An inexpensive two-drawer one will suffice and you can use the extra space to clear up any publishing business clutter that may still be lying around. Whatever you do, though, try not to make filling orders too complex, or you will not enjoy it. Since you are sending out books that are already paid for, you need to need to take some joy in that.

INVOICES

You can have invoices made to order at a stationary store or make them yourself on the computer. Many word processing programs have templates already made up for you to fill in the blanks. You can also buy an in expensive invoice book and hand write them. The advantage to that is that you have an identical copy. It is easy to forget to print two copies of an invoice if you have little or no business experience. Whichever way you decide to do it, you will need invoices in order to have a paper trail while selling your books.

Your business name, address, phone number, FAX number, e-mail address, and website need to be printed on the invoice. Do not forget to write this information on the top of the blank invoices if you decide to use a pre-printed book. It might be a good investment to have a stamp made up with this information on it. Invoices usually have a space for date, order number, and initials of the person who put the order together. Except for the date, you do not need to fill out the other boxes. Some self-publishers will tell you that you will be identified as a self-publisher if you leave these spaces blank. As long as you

INVOICE

Half Acre Publishng
7311 Bell McKinnon Road
Duncan BC V9L6A8
250-746-3919
FAX: same
halfacre@selfpublishing.ca

SOLD TO:		
	INVOICE NUMBER	
	INVOICE DATE	
	PURCHASE ORDER NO.	
	TERMS	30 days
	SALES PERSON	SDA
	SHIPPED VIA	
	F.O.B.	

SHIPPED TO:

QTY	DESCRIPTION	PRICE	AMOUNT
		SUBTOTAL	0.00
		TAX RATE	
		TAX	0.00
		FREIGHT	
			$0.00
			TOTAL DUE

THANK YOU FOR YOUR BUSINESS!

Figure 6 - Sample Invoice

are selling books, who cares? There is no shame in self-publishing, and wholesalers will buy books from you if their customers want them.

When you receive an order from an individual, payment should be included. It is a tough call as to whether you will accept payment up front or be willing to invoice an individual customer. The answer depends on the volume of books you are selling. To be honest, you may not be selling a lot of books and will be glad to take a chance just to move some of them. It is a personal business decision whether you want to send books out to an individual who has not included payment. You can either take the chance and invoice them, or send a postcard explaining that you require prepayment. In order not to run into this problem too often, make sure your advertising and website are clear on how you handle orders. Tell customers you require prepayment. Should you wait until the cheque clears the bank before processing an order? If you do, it might take a week or two before you can get to it. I have never had a cheque bounce on me yet, but that does not mean it will never happen. Depending on the price of your book, it might not be worthwhile to go after an individual. You will have to pay the fees depositing an NSF cheque, and it is often easier to simply write it off. Like many aspects of business, this is a personal decision.

PAYMENT TERMS

Payment terms have changed in the past few years. It used to be acceptable to demand payment in 30 days, but today 60 days is more the norm. Overdue receivables can pose a problem for a small business. Do you let it go 90-120 days or do you charge a penalty after 60 days? If you decide to tack on interest (usually 2% per month), make sure the customer is aware of it. Not that it will make a difference in some cases. Often you will receive the payment after 60 days without the penalty amount added on. The truth is, there is no sense trying to collect it. Some businesses do not pay in 60 days and they expect you to go along with that. This kind of business practice is not just found in the publishing sector either. All retail markets are having to put up with it. It seems that retailers are expecting to keep an item on consignment for a couple of months before paying. The attitude is that you should be grateful to have a place to sell your product. This is not a worthwhile battle for an independent publisher to take on. Even the large trade publishers will not do it.

CONSIGNMENT

These days it seems that more and more booksellers want independently published books to be placed in their stores on consignment. That means they do not pay you unless they sell your books. I find this practice appalling. In the regular retail business, goods are purchased at a wholesale price and sold at a retail price. Goods do not go into stores on consignment. By giving standard industry discounts, a bookseller receives your books at a "wholesale" price and sells for retail. Self-publishers have spent many hours hashing out the question of whether to put books out on consignment or not, but it needs discussion here.

The main reason booksellers want your books on consignment is because they do not want to spend either the time or money to start an account for a one-book publisher. The other main reason is that self-published books tend to be poorly designed both inside and out. They do not sell well because of this flaw, so they sit on the shelf a long time. They are also often geared to a select niche market and that makes them harder to sell. While this does not mean no one will buy your book, it means it will sit on the shelf longer than general books until it finds a market. Small independent booksellers cannot afford to have capital tied up in long term sales. The large chains simply refuse to carry books that they do not believe will sell quickly. In order to get your books into established bookstores, you might not have a choice but to accept a consignment agreement.

A consignment agreement is a contract between you and the bookseller. You need to spell out the terms of the sale. What discount will you give? Since you are not being paid up front, 20-25% is a reasonable discount. A big question to have answered is how long the book-seller will carry your books without payment being made. If you have a narrow market, or you have not gathered a reasonable amount of pub-licity, your book could sit there for a year. That is a long time to have product tied up somewhere and not making money. Six to eight months should be the maximum amount of time to keep a book somewhere on consignment. The reality is that if your book is not selling in a particular location, it is time to move it somewhere else. The longer you leave it in the store, the greater the chance of damage by customers who look at it. At some point the book is not worth anything anymore and you will get it back anyway.

The best way to have any chance that a book-seller will actually purchase your books is to make sure they are designed to meet industry standards. This was discussed in detail in Chapters Two and Four. Put together a great mar-keting package and give the booksellers their dis-counts, as explained in Chapters Six and Seven. This is how the professionals present their prod-ucts. They do not have a problem with books being taken on consignment only. Throughout this book I have mentioned the need for professionalism many times. If you want to compete with the trade publishers, you have to be prepared to play by their rules. Packaging and marketing are two major ones. Attention to detail can see your sales to booksellers become a reality.

CHAPTER NINE
More Possibilities

*People say we're opportunistic, and I hope
so. I think that's a compliment"*
– Samuel Belzberg
Corporate Head and Corporate Raider

AFTERWARD

Now that you are an experienced self-publisher, what can you do next? If you have written non-fiction, you have many possibilities to sell material or spin-offs. You are now viewed as an expert in your field and can use that to start a career in public speaking about your topic. If you are a fiction writer, you can serialize your book. You can also give public readings and become involved with writer's events. It does carry a nice ring to be known as a *novelist* rather than an *author*. Many people aspire to write a novel and the phrase defines you a little more clearly. Whatever you have written, do not stop now that you are published. There are ways to make your material work, and hopefully make money, for you for some time to come.

SELLING RIGHTS

Serialization works well for both fiction and non-fiction. There are two ways to handle it. You can approach magazines and newspapers before you release your book and offer them *first serial rights*. This means you are offering them the right to publish the material for the first time in any publication, **including your book**. Often the contract will specify "North American" or "Canadian" rights. You will be paid and it will generate a large amount of pre-publicity about your book. The book can be serialized in installments or you can write an excerpt for the publication. It is important that the publication has exclusive rights to the material. They are paying for this and you cannot have it printed in other publications at the same time. The operative word here is "first".

Second serial rights are basically reprint rights. This material would come out after your book is released. It is not as sought after or well paid, but it is great publicity. Since these rights are non-exclusive, they can be licensed to several publications.

Electronic rights cover everything from online magazines and databases to CD-ROM magazine anthologies and interactive games. Make sure the contract specifies which electronic media are included. Since there is so much controversy about electronic rights, I highly recommend you have any contract looked at by a lawyer before you sign it. Actually, this is a good practice for any contracts within the business. You are not a publishing business expert and need to seek guidance.

Broadcast rights allow your material to be used on the radio. You might even be asked to put together a one or two minute broadcast using your material. While it is a limited source, if your book has enough depth, you should have sufficient material to keep your name in the public realm for a few weeks or months.

Foreign rights are those you sell outside of Canada and can be either *English language* or *translation rights*. If you prefer, you can sell English language reprint rights for a certain territory. This would mean an area such as the Commonwealth or a specific country such as Great Britain. Translation rights will allow the publisher to sell to any country speaking that language. Do not expect to be able to limit the territory, because it would not be lucrative enough for a foreign publisher. To sell foreign rights, it might be prudent to find an agent who is familiar with this aspect of publishing.

Merchandising rights, or licensing rights, means the right to have any commercial reproduction of your words, illustrations, or characters made into merchandise to be sold. This is done in a big way, usually if a character becomes very popular. Merchandise also normally targets the children's audience. If you are a children's writer or an illustrator, investigate this avenue. It can not only give your book longevity, but it can also satisfy the public's hunger for new toys for their children.

ARTICLES

Now that you are considered to be an expert in your field, you can publish articles about your topic for both magazines and newspapers. There are writers in Canada who make a living from the freelance market. Articles can also be "recycled" by changing the slant of the material. Using this time honoured freelancer's trick, you can sell many articles to many different types of publications. Whether you want to go that route or simply bring attention to yourself and your book, there are some rules to follow in the article writing field.

Articles have a fairly defined format. They begin with an *introduction* or "hook" used to peak the reader's interest. The hook can be as short as one sentence or as long as two paragraphs. Right after that comes the *statement* so that the reader understands what the article is about. This is only one or two sentences long. The main part of your article is the *body*. It should be full of anecdotes and information. This is what your reader wants to know. Finish the article with a *resolution* of one or two paragraphs that ties back to the introduction.

When you decide which magazines you want to send articles to, the first things you will need to do is order their guidelines. You can also find guidelines for many publications at **www.writersdigest.com**. Read them carefully so you know what the editor is looking for. If it is apparent you have no idea what the magazine wants, your work will not be accepted. Buy or borrow copies of any that you are interested in and read them. Actually, you should study them to get a feel for the way they want articles written. If you feel that you can emulate their writing style, send a query letter. I will not go into depth about query letters. There are books and courses available to help you write them. If your idea is accepted, take all the guidance from the editor that you can get. You are a book author and will need mentoring until you are better at writing articles.

Never miss a deadline. If you do, your reputation will be destroyed. Those of us who self-publish actually have not had to deal with too many deadlines along the way. That is not how it is when you have an editor to answer to. They expect professionalism, and that means bringing the material in on time.

PUBLIC SPEAKING

Many authors have become successful public speakers. Sometimes they make a good income too. If you are comfortable with speaking in public, you can talk about your subject. You can speak to service clubs, church groups, libraries, professional organizations, or civic groups. With some determination and imagination, you could set up a speaking circuit that would keep you busy for some time. Whenever there is an opportunity, try to have the media cover your lecture for further publicity.

You want to be prepared when you give public talks. The most obvious thing is to have enough books on hand. It is better to bring too many than to run out. Write an introduction for the person who will be introducing you. That way it is accurate. You will also want to have a poster of your book so it is visible even to the people in the back of the room. Do not forget to bring any marketing material such as bookmarks or postcards. You might also want to make up fliers with order forms in case someone is not sure if they are ready to make a purchase. Do not pressure customers. They will appreciate being given time to think about buying. This might even end up in multiple purchases. Bring change and, if you take credit cards, bring the machine and slips. Many times, you will sell more than one book to a customer if you can accept a credit card. If you are speaking in another town or city, make sure the local bookstores carry your book so it is available after you have gone.

WORKSHOPS AND SEMINARS

Once you have written and published a book, you can use it as a platform to begin teaching about your topic. I conduct workshops about self-publishing and marketing books. These day-long workshops give me an opportunity to introduce self-publishing to people, meet some of my readers, and add to my bank account. I am comfortable teaching and have training in that area.

When you prepare for a workshop or seminar, you first have to develop an outline. This allows you to see visually what material you want to cover. You may find it is either too much or too little for the time you are allowed. If it is too much, consider a narrower aspect of your topic. If it is too little, go back to your book to find more material to "flesh it out". Having your workshop outlined will make it easier for you to organize both your material and any resources you will need. Whether you prefer to use a chalkboard, an overhead projector, or a PowerPoint presentation on a computer, you need to be organized. If you are not well prepared, your audience will have doubts about your ability and that will raise doubts about your knowledge. A good workshop presenter should exude a sense of assurance. After all, if you are now the "expert" on the subject, you should be able to present it with confidence.

Beforehand, contact the facility where you are giving your workshop or seminar to make sure you know where the room is and who will let you in the building. Make sure the coordinator is clear about what you need in the room such as chairs and tables. If there is going to be coffee and tea available, find out who supplies it. Well in advance, give the facility coordinator all material you require to have photocopied, and make sure you write down clearly how many copies you will need. We often conduct workshops in the evening or on a weekend and the staff who do the photocopying do not usually work at those times. Planning ahead is an important part of being organized.

I prefer to use a three-column table format for my outline. The first column gives the main teaching points, the second column covers information I want to remember to present, and the third column is for notes where I list my handouts and when to use transparencies. I also use it to make notes and jot down student questions. The illustration on page 181 shows the format I used for one workshop. You can find many books on the subject of giving workshops and seminars, and you can subscribe to online newsletters. It is not difficult, though, if you plan ahead

DEVELOPING BOOK MARKETING MATERIAL

1. The Book as a Marketing Tool

	30 minutes	Notes
Introduction	Put up book publishing facts. Point out that we compete for shelf space so we have to make out book look like all others.	Facts OHP and handouts
	Your best marketing tool is your book. In order to benefit from this marketing tool, you have to make it look professional. Books that do not look like the others scream "Amateur" and don't get either reviewed or purchased. We compete with the trade publishers for shelf space.	
	Professional design is important. Most book purchasers like the book to look "normal". Give detail on book design. (Prelim, body, back matter) Make sure you give the CIP subject properly. Check bookstores for similar books and copy them.	OHP and handout on design features
	Give example of poorly designed book vs improved design.	OHP of 8 Flags Vol 1 and 2
	Cover and back blurb. 7 seconds to sell the book. You must use all your writing skills to tell about your book in a few bullets. Testimonials and reviews. Read back covers of books in either the library or bookstore. Covers must photograph well in b/w for catalogues and ads. Briefly discuss title choices, including a sub-title.	OHP of Quadra as an example Q&Q cover article
	Dan Pointer has a template worksheet for designing the back cover of your book. It might be helpful.	Handout and OHP
	That being said... Dan Pointer wrote a book about Frisbees and had it designed to look like one. But he was not marketing to bookstores. You have to have the right subject and the right marketing plan to do something like this. Not recommended for first timers.	Page 103
Conclusion	Unless you are a graphic artist and can get away with it, follow accepted format to design a book. Whether we like it or not, people in the book industry prefer books to look like...well books.	Catalogues

Figure 7

and organize everything. After your first workshop or seminar, you will want to make some changes to the material or format. This will only perfect your presentation and draw larger groups to hear it.

BOOKLETS AND REPORTS

These are also called "spin-offs" and can generate a lot of income for the non-fiction writer. You could even make a living selling booklets. There are actually people who do. Because you are the expert, and you wrote the book, you can market any part or piece of it that you wish. Remember, you own the copyright and it is not plagiarism if you use your own text word for word.

Typical booklets are short, from five pages to sixty-four. They can be printed on a high speed photocopier and stapled at the fold. They are not intended to ever sit on a bookstore shelf, so you do not need to worry about a spine. The cover can be made from card stock. They are used to either give more detailed information about a segment of your material or condense something that is very detailed.

A report is short and printed on 8-1/2" x 11" paper. A report with more than one sheet, can be stapled at the corner. It can be a resource list or detailed bibliography or a kit or just about anything that you think a reader might want to have more information about. Letters and requests from your fans can point you in the direction of what materials might be turned into a good report. You can mail these folded in #10 envelopes with a first class stamp.

Booklets and reports can be advertised in the back of your book, on your website, or in the classified section of periodicals that relate to the topic of your book. They can be sold as direct sales which I explain in Chapter Seven or be given away. If you plan to send it free of charge, you can do it one of two ways. One way is to request a self-addressed stamped envelope (SASE) in order to defray your costs. The other way is to use it as a promotional item. Offer it for free if the customer purchases your book (or a certain number of them) or fills out an online form. The latter will allow you to build a database for future marketing. Booklets can become a serious part of your publishing business.

AWARDS

Nothing makes your book stand out more than winning an award. You become instantly well-known in Canadian literary circles, and your books will each carry a sticker announcing the win. Sales will increase because people always want to read award winning books. You will find it beneficial to announce this in all your marketing literature. It can even cause a resurgence in interest in your book. While most self-published books do not qualify, there are still awards out there that you will qualify for. Study the list in the appendix.

The first thing you need to do is go to the website or write to the organization and ensure your book is suitable for entry. Send the book or books with a self-addressed and stamped post card requesting receipt information so you know it has arrived safely. I cannot stress enough the importance of reading entry guidelines thoroughly. Here is that professional angle I have talked about before. If you miss out on something, you will be viewed as a self-published amateur. This is not good publicity for either yourself or others.

Writer's Digest magazine runs the Annual International Self-Published Book Awards every year. You submit your book in December and the winners are announced the following summer. There is a grand prize winner and several categories to choose from. While it does cost $100 (US) for the first book and $50 (US) for additional entries, the grand prize is $2500(US), a marketing plan from Dan Poynter, promotion in *Writer's Digest* and *Publisher's Weekly*, and copies of the winner's books sent to ten major review houses with a guaranteed review in *Midwest Book Review*. Category winners will each receive $500 (US) and promotion in *Writer's Digest*. All winners will also receive book jacket seals along with promotion on the magazine's website. All honourable mentions are listed in the summer edition of the magazine when they announce the winners. It is not cheap to enter, but offers an opportunity to have your book read by a serious editor. If you win anything, the cost of entry then becomes moot.

TRADE PUBLISHERS

Once you have successfully self-published a book, trade publishers will find you more interesting. If you would rather have someone else publish your books in the future, you are now considered a reasonable risk. After all, you did it once and proved that you are capable of writing a book from start to finish. You now have a "name" and are no longer a complete unknown. You understand the publishing business and will be able to help, rather than hinder, your publishing house's attempts to market your book. If you made the rounds and received either silence or rejection slips, this could very well be your "calling card" to finding a publisher receptive to your next manuscript.

The other side of the coin is if your book is so wildly successful, and you cannot keep up with print runs, you want to find a publisher to buy the rights to publish your book. If this happens, you will be famous and making a lot of money. You can make a deal with the trade publisher that will give you a larger royalty than the average author makes. Or you can partner with a publisher to co-publish the book. This will require an extensive contract which will need to be seen by a lawyer.

REMAINDERS

Sometimes a book does not sell well and other times it simply runs its course. When you find that you have been storing boxes of books for a few years, it might be time to investigate the remainders market. If you have ever been to a bookstore with older but unused books, they are probably remainders. Remainder sellers often show up in malls with tables of books. Try not to think of the remainder market as the demise of your book. It is actually a way to give new life to an old product.

Remainders dealers throughout North America receive at least a 70-80% discount. This may mean you receive only the cost of producing the book. That is better than receiving nothing. It is definitely better than storing hundreds, or even thousands, of books in your basement or garage. Remember, this is a product and needs to be moved out. If you plan to write and publish another book, you will need the room. If you are tired of the whole project, you do not want it staring at you day after day. If you are prepared to put your business hat on, you will see that sending books off to a remainders dealer is simply a business decision. Not that you have to, of course. You may want to keep all of your books and continue to sell them for the rest of your life. They belong to you and you can do whatever you want to do with them. But it is nice to know that if you do not want to store them anymore, there is an avenue for sales.

CHAPTER TEN
Success Stories

*You are born with two things: existence
and opportunity, and these are the raw
materials out of which you can make
a successful life.*
– Charles Templeton
Jack-of-All-Trades

We often believe that good things will never happen to us. We think that only "others" will win the lottery or find a business that makes them rich. This chapter is about average people, like you and me, who found a niche and worked hard to make their books into best sellers. Admittedly, they are all non-fiction books, but with the upsurge in self-publishing, it will not be long before we see more fiction hitting the bestseller lists.

Studying successful people is one way to understand how they got that way. That is why biographies and autobiographies of the rich and

famous sell so well. We want to be wildly successful and wonder if we emulate them, will we also
have success. I have touched on some of the most
successful self-publishers in Canada. To learn more
about the people and their achievements, visit
their websites.

Jean Paré

Books: *Company's Coming* cookbooks series
Number sold: 20 Million+
Website: **www.companyscoming.com**

The most successful self-publisher in Canada,
Jean Paré was an Alberta caterer who merely tried
to fill a gap for requests for some of her recipes. She
published *150 Delicious Squares* and travelled
through the province to find retailers to take them.
As more people wanted more recipes, she wrote
more cookbooks. Today the *Company's Coming*
series has more than 60 titles. Total sales have sur-
passed 20 million books. The company she co-
founded with her son is operated by family members, giving Jean Paré plenty of time to work with
the staff in the test kitchen. She is involved in all
aspects of recipe development to ensure the continued quality we have come to trust from her books.

David Chilton

Book: *The Wealthy Barber*
Number of book sold: 2 million+
Website: **www.wealthybarber.com**

Dave Chilton started by hiring a consulting firm to help him prepare the book – and he wisely followed their advice. He took a year off work to travel and promote his book. Self-published in his basement, he sold 12,000 copies in the first two months alone. He is a shrewd businessman who made smart deals with publishers and corporations. According to one report, he believes in the need for an order form at the back of the book. He discovered that people actually order more books when there is one. He took this self-publishing business seriously and it made him into the successful author and speaker he is today.

Greta and Janet Podleski

Book: *Looney Spoons: Low-fat made fun!*
Number sold: 800,000+
Book: *CrazyPlates: Low-fat food so good, you'll swear it's bad for you!*
Number sold: 500,000+
Website: **www.crazyplates.com**

Ontario sisters, Janet and Greta Podleski, are a determined pair of women. They believed so strongly in their funny approach to a low-fat cookbook that they put everything they had into getting it published. Greta moved in with Janet and her husband, they quit their jobs and maxed out their credit cards. They even sold many of their possessions to raise the money to make this project work. The story of selling Janet's wedding dress at a lawn sale is a true one.

David Chilton invested in the book and put his well honed marketing skills behind it. The rest, as they say, is history. After one appearance on *The Today Show*, their book was #1 on Ingram's cookbook bestseller list. Today the partners have seen successful with a second cookbook which was a national #1 bestseller and a 2001 finalist for the James Beard Foundation Cookbook awards.

Joe Garner

Books: *Never Fly Over An Eagle's Nest*
Never A Time To Trust
Never Chop Your Rope
Never Under The Table
Never Forget The Good Times
Number sold: approximately 300,000+

The late Joe Garner's success was due primarily to his tenacity as a salesman. At the age of 71, the British Columbia writer self-published his first book, and it went on to sell more than 100,000 copies over the next 15 years. He packed his van with 1500 copies and drove across Canada selling them along the way. He spoke at libraries, in bookstores, on the radio, and at every service club that would have him. He was so successful that he even had to have more books printed and shipped to him in Calgary on the way back. Beating the odds, his second book also became a bestseller. He started his final book at the age of 84. Even though he suffered a stroke while writing it, he continued to work on it. He wrote books because he wanted to tell his stories and give his readers pleasure. He even once admitted that writing was part of what kept him alive.

Dania Lebovics
Books: *Kiddy Chronicles* (no longer available)
  Baby Chronicles
  School Year Chronicles
  Les chroniques de Bebe
  Les chroniques des Annes d'ecole
Number sold: 100,000+
Website: **www.babychronicles.com**

Dania Lebovics first *Kiddy Chronicles* was one she made for herself to chronicle the events in her child's life. She made some as gifts for friends, and then phone calls started coming from people who had seen them and wanted one. Her first three editions were designed on her home computer and printed at the local copy shop. She had them bound professionally and placed on consignment in baby and maternity stores. She used up the family savings and then decided to take a chance on future editions. This chance paid off as you can see by the number of copies of books sold to date. At present she is working on a Spanish edition called *Cronicas del bebe*.

Virginia Brucker

Book: *Gifts From the Heart: 450 Simple Ways to Make Your Family's Christmas More Meaningful*

Number sold: 17,000+

Website: **www3.telus.net/webelieve/**

When cancer struck a staff member and the parents of two students at a small British Columbia school, teacher Virginia Brucker believed she had to do something. What she did was create a book with imaginative ways to celebrate the Christmas season without spending a lot of money. She wanted to use the book as a way to raise money for the Canadian Cancer Society. With the help of school staff and students, she had the book ready to go in three years. Even the cover artwork came from a 10-year-old student.

Available mainly online, by phone or mail, twenty-five percent of the profits are donated to the Cancer Society. Groups that use the book for a fundraiser receive another forty percent. So far, more than $70,000 has been donated to the Cancer Society. *Gifts From the Heart* has been written about in the *Ottawa Citizen* and *Canadian Living* magazine. The Canadian Centre for Philanthropy published a whole page praising the author and her husband for their dedication and volunteer work.

One of the main things you will learn from reading about these successful self-publishers is that they have tenacity and courage. It takes a lot of courage to quit your job or take a long leave of absence. It takes courage to clean out the family's savings account, max out credit cards, or remortgage your home. It takes courage to start any kind of business, much less a self-publishing one. And it takes an incredible amount of courage to give interviews and speak publicly about your book. All these successful self-publishers possess a rare courage that has allowed them to follow this dream.

Something all of these authors have in common is that they were willing to "bang the drum" about their book. They toured and they spoke and they interviewed and they did whatever it took to bring their books to the attention of the buying public. Along the way, you can be sure they made mistakes. But they learned from their mistakes and kept right on going. This is the true entrepreneurial spirit.

Self-publishing is both demanding and gratifying. It is time consuming, costs money, and has its own idiosyncrasies. It is easy to print a book, but more complex to market one. It takes guts and determination. None of Canada's successful self-publishers fell into success. They made it themselves. You can achieve success too, if you have the right product and a positive attitude. I wish every one of you good luck in your publishing endeavours. Make use of the resources I have listed in the appendices and visit my website at **www.selfpublishing.ca** for great links and up to date information. Maybe a future edition of this book will feature you and your book as a success story.

APPENDIX A
CHECKLIST

TO DO	DONE	DATE
Pick a business name		
Register the business		
Receive a business number (BN)		
Open business account at the bank		
Research *Books in Print* for a title		
Choose a title		
Choose a publication date		
Design cover		
Write back cover material		
Order ISBN		
Order Cataloguing in Publication (CIP) information		
Order a barcode		
Register with Canadian Books in Print (CBIP)		
Register with RR Bowker		
Have the manuscript edited		
Proofread manuscript and make corrections		
Organize illustrations and write cutlines		
Get 3-7 printer estimates		
Write a marketing plan		
Write blurbs		
Write an information sheet		
Write news releases		
Make up a media package		
Put up a website		
Send book(s) to Legal Deposit		
Re-read chapter 7 and sell books		

APPENDIX B

ISBN AND CIP AGENTS FOR CANADIAN TRADE PUBLISHERS

1. For ISBN numbers:
   Canadian ISBN Agency
   National Library of Canada
   395 Wellington Street
   Ottawa, ON K1A 0N4
   Tel: (819) 994-6872 FAX: (819) 997-7517
   E-mail: **isbn@nlc-bnc.ca**

2. The National CIP office:
   CIP Coordinator
   National Library (see address above)
   Tel: (819) 994-6881 FAX: (819) 997-7517
   E-mail: **cip@nlc-bnc.ca**
   Website: **www.nlc-bnc.ca/cip/**

3. For publishers in Alberta, British Columbia,
   and the Territories:
   CIP Office
   Library Processing Centre - Catalogue Branch

2206 East Mall
University of British Columbia
Vancouver, BC V6T 1Z8
Tel: (604) 822-6838 FAX: (604) 822-4789
E-mail: **cip@unixg.ubc.ca**
Website: **www.library.ubc.ca/cip/cip.html**

4. For publishers in Manitoba and Saskatchewan:
    CIP Office
    Technical Services
    Elizabeth Dafoe Library
    University of Manitoba
    Winnipeg, MB R3T 2N2
    Tel: (204) 474-9476 FAX: (204) 474-7596
    E-mail: **parting@bldgdafoe.lan1.umanitoba.ca**

5. For publishers in Ontario
    (excluding the Ottawa area):
    CIP Office
    University of Toronto Library
    7th Floor, Room 7039
    130 St. George Street
    Toronto, ON M5S 1A5
    Tel: (416) 978-1803 FAX: (416) 978-7457

6. For publishers in the Ottawa area and
    English-
    language publishers in Quebec:
    CIP Office
    Acquisitions and Bibliographic Services
    National Library of Canada (see address above)

Tel: (819) 994-6881 FAX: (819) 997-7517
E-mail: **cip@nlc-bnc.ca**
Website: **www.nlc-bnc.ca/cip/**

7. For French language publishers in Quebec:
   Responsable CIP
   Bibliotheque nationale du Quebec
   2275, rue Holt
   Montreal, QC H2G 3H1
   Tel: (514) 873-1100, ext 375 FAX: (514) 873-4310
   E-mail: **SRousseau@Biblionat.gouv.OC.CA**
   Website: **www.biblinat.gouv.qc.ca/texte/t0021.htm**

8. For publishers in the Atlantic provinces:
   CIP Office
   Cataloguing Department
   Killam Library
   Dalhousie University
   Halifax, NS B3H 4H8
   Tel: (902) 494-6687 FAX: (902) 494-3576
   E-mail: **tremblay@is.dal.ca**

APPENDIX C

BUSINESS SERVICE CENTRES

Business Number:
Business Window located at nearest Canada
Cutstoms and Revenue Agency office:
(613) 957-8109
1-800-959-5525
www.ccra-adrc.gv.ca
Forms to request registration for a business
number are at this site.

Business Development Bank of Canada
To find nearest BDC office:
1-888-INFOBDC (463-6242)
www.bdc.ca

Canada Business Service Centres:
www.cbsc.org
Click on your provincial/territorial flag at the
bottom of the homepage for information on registering business name.

Provincial/Territorial Canada Business Service Centre offices:

Canada/Nova Scotia Business Service Centre
1575 Brunswick St
Halifax, NS B3J 2G1
(902) 426-8604
1-800-668-1010
E-mail: halifax@cbsc.ic.gc.ca

Canada/New Brunswick Canada Business
Service Centre
570 Queen St
Ground Floor, Barker House
Fredericton, NB E3B 6Z6
(506) 444-6140
1-800-668-1010
E-mail: cbscn@cbsc.ic.gc.ca

Canada/Prince Edward Island Canada Business
Service Centre
75 Fitzroy Street
Ground Floor
Charlottetown, PE C1A 7K2
(902) 368-0771
1-800-668-1010
E-mail: pei@cbsc.ic.gc.ca

Canada/Newfoundland & Labrador Business
Service Centre
90 O'Leary Avenue

St. John's, NF A1B 3T1
(709) 772-6022
1-800-668-1010
E-mail:info@cbsc.ic.gc.ca

Info entrepreneurs
5 Place Ville-Marie
Suite 125000
Montreal, QC H3B 4Y2
(514) 496-INFO (4636)
1-800-322-INFO

Canada/Ontario Canada Business Service Centre
230 Richmont St. West, 9th Floor
Toronto, ON M5V 3E5
(416) 775-3456
1-800-567-2345
E-mail:ontario@cbsc.ic.gc.ca

Canada Business Service Centre
250-240 Graham Avenue
Winnipeg, MB R3C 4B3
(204) 984-2272
1-800-665-2019
E-mail: manitoba@cbsc.ci.gc.ca

Canada/Saskatchewan Canada Business
Service Centre
(306) 956-2323
1-800-667-4374

The Business Link Canada Business Service
Centre
10237-104 Street NW, Suite 100
Edmonton, AB T5J 1B1
(403) 422-7722
1-800-272-9675

Canada/British Columbia Canada Business
Service Centre
601 West Cordova St
Vancouver, BC V6B 1G1
(604) 775-5525
1-800-667-2272
www.smallbusinessbc.ca

Canada/Nunavit Business Service Centre
PO Box 1000, Stn 1198
Parnaivik Building
Iqaluit, Nunavit X0A 0H0
(867) 979-6813
1-877-499-5199
E-mail: cnbsc@gov.nu.ca

Canada/Northwest Territories Business Service
Centre
Scotia Centre, 8th Floor
PO Box 1320
Yellowknife, NT X1A 2L9
(403) 873-7958
1-800-661-0599
E-mail: yel@cbsc.ci.gc.ca

Canada/Yukon Canada Business Service Centres
101-307 Jarvis Street
Whitehorse, YK Y1A 2H3
(403) 633- 6257
1-800-661-0543
E-mail:yukon@cbsc.ci.gc.ca

APPENDIX D

CANADIAN BARCODE SUPPLIERS

1. AURORA Bar Code Technologies Ltd
   10310 - 176 Street NW, Ste 200
   Edmonton, AB T5S 1L3
   (780) 483-6025 or 1-800-689-7696
   FAX: (780) 484-8767
   sales@aurorabarcode.com
   www.aurorabarcode.com

   Calgary office
   Tel: (403) 266-7455
   salescgy@aurorabarcode.com

   British Columbia office
   4363 Dawson Street, Ste 200
   Burnaby, BC V5C 4B4
   (604) 293-1130 or 1-888-869-2201
   FAX: (604) 293-0291
   salesbc@aurorabarcode.com

2. Barcode Graphics Inc
   30 Dohme Avenue
   Toronto, ON M4B 3M4
   (416) 751-1474 or 1-888-263-3669

FAX: (416) 751-1575
info@barcodegraphics.com
www.barcodegraphics.com

3. Barcode Systems
   1475 King Edward Street
   Winnipeg, MB R3H 0R7
   (204) 985-1510 or 1-800-310-7226
   FAX: (204) 985-1520
   service@bsidirect.com
   www.bsidirect.com

4. Batten Graphics
   543 Richmond Street W, Ste 125
   Toronto, ON M5V 1Y6
   (416) 703-1355
   FAX: (416) 703-4427

5. Dyna Graphics
   1308 Seymour Street
   Vancouver, BC V6B 3P3
   (604) 684-4561
   FAX: (604) 684-3882
   dyna@direct.ca
   www.dynaprint.com

6. Fine Line Bar-Code Technologies
   2600-T Skymark Avenue, Unit 103
   Missisauga, ON LW4 5B2
   (905) 629-4336 or 1-800-465-1890
   FAX: (905) 629-7714

7. Ingenieuse Productions
   Edmonton, AB
   bar code film masters
   (780) 974-7491
   FAX: (780) 426-7183
   ingenieuse@telusplanet.net
   www.netsnational.com

8. Symbol Imaging
   225 Jarvis Street
   Toronto, ON M5B 2C1
   (312) 664-0700 or 1-800-662-0701
   FAX: (312) 664-3949
   sales@barcode-us.com
   www.barcode-us.com

APPENDIX E
BOOK CONTESTS AND AWARDS

The following are book awards and competitions available to Canadian writers. Many provincial awards are only open to residents of that province. For more detailed information, either contact the organization directly or see the latest issue of *The Canadian Writer's Market*. An on-line site to find information about Canadian contests is **http://www.ncf.ca/~ab297/contests.html**, which is privately maintained.

1. Alberta New Fiction Competition
   Alberta Community Development,
   Arts & Cultural Industries Branch
   3rd Floor, Beaver House,
   10158 - 103rd Street,
   Edmonton, AB T5J 0X6
   Deadline: December 1

2. Alberta Writing for Youth Competition
   See 1 (above) for address
   Deadline: December

3. The Alden Nowlan Award
   Arts Branch, New Brunswick Department
   of Municipalities, Culture & Housing
   P.O. Box 6000,
   Fredericton, NB E3B 5H1
   Deadline: June 15

4. Ann Connor Brimer Award
   Linda Hodgins, Dartmouth Regional Library,
   60 Alderney Drive,
   Dartmouth, NS B2Y 4P8
   Deadline: April 30

5. Arthur Ellis Awards
   Secretary/Treasurer, Crime Writers of Canada
   P.O. Box 113, 3007 Kingston Road,
   Scarborough, ON M1M 1P1
   Deadline: December 31

6. Authors' Awards
   Periodical Marketers of Canada
   175 Bloor Street E., Ste 1007, South Tower,
   Toronto, ON M4W 2R8
   Deadline: July 31

7. The B.C. Book Prizes
   Alan Twigg, B.C. BookWorld
   3516 West 13th Avenue (rear),
   Vancouver, BC V6R 2S3
   Deadline: December

8. B.C. Gas Lifetime Achievement Award
   See 9 (below) for address

9. B.C. Historical Federation Writing
   Competition
   c/o P. McGeachie
   7953 Rosewood Street,
   Burnaby, BC V5E 2H4
   Deadline: December 15

10. The pbNichol Chapbook Award
    The Phoenix Community Works Foundation
    316 Dupont Street,
    Toronto, ON M5R 1V9
    Deadline: March 31

11. The Bronwen Wallace Award
    c/o The Writers' Development Trust
    24 Ryerson Avenue, Ste 201,
    Toronto, ON M5T 2P3
    Deadline: January 31

12. Canadian Authors Association Awards
    Jeffrey Holmes
    275 Slater Street, Ste 500,
    Ottawa, ON K1P 5H9

    Air Canada Award
    Deadline: April

The Vicky Metcalf Body of Work Award
Deadline: December 31

CAA Literary Awards
Deadline: December 15

13. Canadian Historical Association Awards
Joanne Mineault
395 Wellington Street,
Ottawa, ON K1A 0N3

The Wallace K. Ferguson Award
Deadline: December 15

Sir John A. Macdonald Prize
Deadline: December 15

14. Canadian Library Association Book Awards
CLA Membership Services
200 Elgin Street, Ste 602,
Ottawa, ON 2P 1L5

Book of the Year for Children Award
Young Adult Canadian Book Award

15. City of Dartmouth Book Award
Charby Slernin, c/o Dartmouth
Regional Library
60 Alderney Drive,
Dartmouth, NS B2Y 4P8
Deadline: December

16. City of Toronto Book Awards
    Richard Frank, c/o City Clerk's Department,
    Communications Division
    22nd Floor, East Tower, City Hall,
    Toronto, ON M5H 2N2
    Deadline: January 30

17. City of Vancouver Book Award
    Russell Kelly
    See 9 for address
    Deadline: June

18. Dafoe Book Prize
    J.E. Rea, Department of History,
    University of Manitoba
    500 Dysart Road,
    Winnipeg, MN R3T 2M8

19. Edna Staebler Award for Creative
    Non-Fiction
    Office of the President,
    Wilfrid Laurier University
    75 University Avenue W.,
    Waterloo, ON N2L 3C5
    Deadline: May 19

20. Gabrielle Roy Prize
    Joe Pivato, Athabasca University,
    Learning Centre - Edmonton
    2nd Floor, North Tower, 7th Street Plaza,
    10030 - 107th Street, Edmonton, AB T5J 3E5

21. Geoffrey Bilson Award for Historical Fiction
for Young People
Jeffrey Canton, Canadian Children's
Book Centre
35 Spadina Road, Toronto, ON M5R 2S9

22. The Giller Prize
Kelly Kelly
21 Steepleview Crescent,
Richmond Hill, ON L4C 9R1

23. The Gordon Montador Award
c/o The Writers' Development Trust
24 Ryerson Avenue, Ste 201,
Toronto, ON M5T 2P3

24. Government of Newfoundland &
Labrador Arts & Letters Competition
Regina Best, Arts and Culture Centre
P.O. Box 1854,
St. John's, NF A1C 5P7
Deadline: March

25. Governor General's Literary Award
Josiane Polidori, Canada Council
P.O. Box 1047, 99 Metcalfe Street,
Ottawa, ON K1P 5V8
Deadline: August 31
(Note: Self-published books are not eligible
for this award, but writing letters to the
Canada Council might change that)

26. The Hawthorne Poetry Award
    Robin Skelton, Hawthorne Society of
    Arts and Letters
    1255 Victoria Avenue,
    Victoria, BC V8S 4P3
    Deadline: March 31

27. IODE National Book Award
    Marty Dalton
    40 Orchard View Boulevard, Ste 254,
    Toronto, ON M4R 1B9
    Deadline: January 31

28. IODE Toronto Book Award
    Catherine Moore
    44 Strath Avenue,
    Etobicoke, ON M8X 1R3
    Deadline: December 1

29. Island Literary Awards
    P.E.I. Council of the Arts
    P.O. Box 2234,
    Charlottetown, PEI C1A 8B9

30. Jewish Book Awards
    Joan Tooke, Jewish Book Awards,
    Koffler Centre of the Arts
    4588 Bathurst Street,
    North York, ON M2R 1W6
    Deadline: February 1

31. League of Canadian Poets Awards
    Sandra Drzewiecki
    54 Wolseley Street, 3rd Floor,
    Toronto, ON M5T 1A5

    Gerald Lampert Memorial Award
    Deadline: January 31

    Pat Lowther Memorial Award
    Deadline: January 31

32. The Lionel Gelber Prize
    Marcia McClung, Applause Communications
    398 Adelaide Street W., Ste 1007,
    Toronto, ON M5V 1S7
    Deadline: July 1

33. The Macpherson Prize
    The Canadian Political Science Association
    1 Stewart Street, Ste 206,
    University of Ottawa,
    Ottawa, ON K1N 6H7
    Deadline: December

34. The Malahat Review Novella Prize
    Marlene Cookshaw, The Malahat Review,
    University of Victoria
    P.O. Box 1700 MS 8524,
    Victoria, BC V8W 2Y2
    Deadline: March 1 (biennially on even years)

35. McNally Robinson Award for the
    Manitoba Book of the Year
    Robyn Maharaj, Manitoba Writers's Guild
    100 Arthur Street, Ste 206,
    Winnipeg, MN 3B 1H3
    Deadline: cember 31

36. Mr. Christie's Book Awards
    Marlene Yustin, c/o Christie Brown and Co.
    2150 Lakeshore Boulevard W.,
    Toronto, ON M8V 1A3
    Deadline: January 31

37. National Business Book Awards
    Arianna Venditti, Coopers & Lybrand
    5160 Yonge Street,
    North York, ON M2N 6L3
    Deadline: Mid-December

38. Ottawa-Carleton Book Award
    Arts Office, Regional Muncipality of
    Ottawa-Carleton
    Ottawa-Carleton Centre, 111 Lisgar Street,
    Ottawa, ON K2P 2L7
    Deadline: anuary 20

39. QSPELL Book Awards
    Jeanne Randle
    1200 Atwater Avenue,
    Montreal, PQ H3Z 1X4
    Deadline: May 31

40. The Ruth Schwartz Children's Book Award
    The Literature Office,
    Ontario Arts Council
    151 Bloor Street W.,
    Toronto, ON M5S 1T6

41. Saskatchewan Writers' Guild Awards
    Paul Wilson
    P.O. Box 3986, Regina, SK S4P 3R9
    Deadline: June

42. The Smiley Prize
    The Canadian Political Science Association
    1 Stewart Street, Ste 206,
    University of Ottawa,
    Ottawa, ON K1N 6H7
    Deadline: December (given biannually)

43. Smithbooks/Books in Canada First
    Novel Award
    Adrian Stein, Publisher, Book in Canada
    130 Spadina Avenue, Ste 603,
    Toronto, ON M5V 2L4
    Deadline: December 31

44. Stephen Leacock Memorial Medal for Humour
    Jean Bradley Dickson
    P.O. Box 854,
    Orillia, ON L3V 6K8
    Deadline: December 31

45. Trillium Book Award
Gartly Wagner, Ministry of Culture,
Tourism and Recreation,
Libraries and Community Information
Branch
77 Bloor Street W., 3rd Floor,
Toronto, ON M7A 2R9
Deadline: November 15/December 15

46. VanCity Book Prize
See 9 for Address
Deadline: May 15

47. Writers' Federation of New Brunswick
Literary Competition
Anna Mae Snider, Writers' Federation of
New Brunswick
103 Church Street, P.O. Box 37, Stn A,
Fredericton, NB E3B 4Y2

48. Writers' Federation of Nova Scotia Awards
Jane Buss
1809 Barrington Street, Ste 901,
Halifax, NS B3J 3K8

Atlantic Writing Competition
Deadline: August 27

Thomas Raddall Atlantic Fiction Award
Deadline: April 15

Evelyn Richardson Memorial Literary
Trust Award
Deadline: April 15

49. Writers Guild of Alberta Annual Awards
c/o Writers Guild of Alberta
11759 Groat Road, 3rd Floor,
Edmonton, AB T5M 3K6
Deadline: December 31

50. The Great Canadian Literary Hunt
c/o THIS Magazine
401 Richmond Street West, Ste 396,
Toronto, ON M5V 3A8

APPENDIX F
ASSOCIATIONS FOR WRITERS

Association of Canadian Publishers
www.publishers.ca

Canadian Authors Association
www.canauthors.org

Canadian Poetry Association
www3.sympatico.ca/cpa/
www.mirrow.org/cpa/

Canadian Society of Children's Authors,
Illustrators & Performers (CANSCAIP)
www.canscaip.org

Crime Writers of Canada
www.crimewriterscanada.com

Federation of British Columbia Writers
www.bcwriters.com

Independent Publishers Association of Canada
www.ipac-publishers.com

Inscribe Christian Writers' Fellowship
www.inscribe.org

Island Writers Association (PEI)
Creative@peinet.pe.ca

League of Canadian Poets
www.poets.ca

Manitoba Writers' Guild Inc.
www.mbwriter.mb.ca

The Ontario Poetry Society
www.mirror/org/tops/

PEN Canada
www.pencanada.ca

Periodical Writers Association of Canada
www.pwac.ca

Professional Editors Association
www.editors.ca

Professional Editors Association of Vancouver
Island
www.peavi.bc.ca

Quebec Writers' Federation
www.qwf.org

Alberta Romance Writers' Association
www.albertaromancewriters.com
Romance Writers of America - Greater
Vancouver Chapter
www.rwagvc.com

Romance Writers of America – Vancouver
Island Chapter
**http://writing.shawguides.com/ARomance
Odyssey/**

Saskatchewan Writers' Guild
www.skwriter.com

SFCanada (Science Fiction Writers)
www.sfcanada.ca

Union des ecrivaines et ecrivains quebecois
www.uneq.qc.ca

Writers' Alliance of Newfoundland and
Labrador
www.writersalliance.nf.ca

The Writers' Federation of New Brunswick
**www.sjfn.nb.ca/community_hall/W/Writers
_Federation_NB/index.htm**

Writers' Federation of Nova Scotia
www.writers.ns.ca

Writers Guild of Alberta
www.writersguild.ab.ca

Writers Guild of Canada
www.writersguildofcanada.com

Writers' Union of Canada
www.writersunion.ca

APPENDIX G
WEBSITES FOR WRITERS AND PUBLISHERS

Booksellers

www.amazon.com
www.authographedbyauthor.com
www.booksamillion.com
www.booksatoz.com
www.cyclopsmedia.com
www.ebookmall.com
www.justbookz.com
www.knowbetter.com
www.lights.com/publisher/ca.html
www.selfpublishingservice.com

Newsletters and magazines

www.bcbookworld.com
    Canada's largest circulation newspaper
    about books
www.forewordmagzine.com
www.independentpublisher.com
www.publishingbasics.com

www.quillandquire.com
  Canada's publishing periodical
www.wexfordpress.com/news/news2.pdf
www.worldwidewriters.com
www.writersdigest.com
  Articles, a newsletter, and a large database
  of publisher's guidelines.
www.writepage.com

General Information and Resources

www.authorlink.com
www.author.co.uk
  SP site in the UK
www.bookwire.com
  Maintained by R.R. Bowker
www.canada.justice.gc.ca/en/cons/jeh/britt.html
www.cbabook.org
  Canadian Booksellers Association
www.cla.ca
  Canadian Library Association
www.parapub.com
  Dan Poynter's site
www.published.com
www.pma-online
  Publishers Marketing Association
www.rtir.com
www.selfpublishing.ca
  Self Publishing in Canada
www.sfwa.org/beware
www.spannet.org
  Small Publishers Association of North

America
www.spawn.org
  Small Publishers, Artists, and Writers
  Network
www.strategis.ic.gc.ca
www.talion.com/presskits.html

Marketing
www.authorsden.com
www.bookbooters.com
www.bookclubdeals.com/canada-book-club.html
www.bookmarket.com
www.publicizeyourbook.com
www.publishinggame.com
www.umbrellabooks.com

GLOSSARY OF PUBLISHING TERMS

AA Author's alterations, the changes made by the author on proofs. Can be costly to the author if there are too many changes.

ABI Advanced Book Information. Publishers supply R.R. Bowker with information about their book which is used to list books in *Forthcoming Books* and *Books in Print*. They prefer you register online, but you can still use the form.

Acid-free paper Paper which will not yellow and will not deteriorate for two hundred years.

Acknowledgment A statement expressing gratitude for contributions to a work by an individual or organization. Part of the book's FRONT MATTER.

Acquisition librarian The librarian who chooses and orders new library books.

Adoptions Books accepted for use as textbooks in schools, colleges, and universities.

Advance An agreed prepayment to the author, paid either before or at the time of publication, to be offset against future royalties.

Advance copies Copies of a publication made up in limited quantity for promotional purposes.

Afterword The author's final remarks to the reader. Part of the book's AFTER MATTER.

AKA "also known as" or an alias. See Pen name and Pseudonym.

Anthology A collection of writings by one or more authors published as a single book.

Appendix A list of resources or other reference material. Part of a book's AFTER MATTER. Plural form is appendices.

Artwork Any illustrative matter such as photographs, illustrations, charts or graphs other than straight text.

As-told-to A book produced by a writer in collaboration with a non writer, usually a celebrity.

Back jacket flap The back inner flap of a dust jacket that often has an author's photo and brief biography.

Backlist Previously published books that are still in print and available from the publisher.

Back matter All pages in a book after the main text such as APPENDICES, GLOSSARY, BIBLIOGRAPHY, or INDEX. Also called END MATTER.

Back order An order for books held until they become available.

Bar code The ISBN and price code that is on the back cover of the book. Called the Bookland 13 EAN.

Bastard title Half title page that is the first page of a book.

Bestseller A top selling book based on bookstore sales.

Biblio A page in the front matter of a book giving details of the publisher and publishing history. Also called the legal page.

Bibliography List of publications providing reference material on the book's subject. Part of the BACK MATTER.

Binding Method of securing the leaves or signatures of a book, brochure or manuscript.

Blank An unprinted page that is part of a signature.

Bleed The part of an image that extends beyond the trim marks on a page.

Blue pencil A special pencil whose marks cannot be reproduced used to make corrections on camera-ready copy.

Blurb A promotional advertisement, announcement or phrase.

Boards Stiff paper in the cover of a hardback book or the camera-ready pasted up copy ready for the printer.

Body The text portion of a book excluding FRONT MATTER and BACK MATTER.

Boldface Type with a heavy, black appearance.

Book A publication of 49 or more pages that is not a serial or periodical.

Bookfair An event where publishers display and sell their books.

Booklet A publication with more pages than a pamphlet and less than a book, usually fewer than 24 pages long.

Book packager A person or company who contracts with publishers to deliver proofs at least to the camera-ready stage. Also called book producers.

Book proofs Page proofs put together in a book form.

Bulk Both the thickness of a sheet of paper and the thickness of a book without its cover.

Bullet A heavy centred dot

CIS Coated One Side. Refers to a book cover stock which is smooth and shiny on one side.

Camera-ready Artwork, copy, or pasteup that is ready to be photographed without alteration.

Caps Capital or uppercase letters.

Caption Descriptive text accompanying an illustration, drawing, table, etc.

Cased/case-bound Hardcover book.

Casting off Calculating the number of typeset pages based on character count.

Chapbook A small book or pamphlet of popular tales, ballads or poems.

Character A single letter, number, punctuation mark, or space.

CIP Cataloging in Publication. A voluntary program, run by the National Library of Canada, whereby Canadian books are catalogued before they are published and the cataloging information is distributed to librarians and booksellers.

Clip art Pictures that can be purchased and used in books instead of having to draw your own.

Clipping service A firm that collects articles, reviews and notices for a fee.

Cloth A material used for casing books.

Coated paper Paper stock with a white clay surface for smooth printing.

Collating Gathering sheets together in proper order.

Colour correction Any method used to improve colour rendition such as masking, dot etching and scanning.

Colour printing Any print colour except black on white paper.

Colour separation Camera technique of separating each of the four primary colours for the four necessary printing plates.

Comb binding A plastic multi-pronged binding that allows a book to lie flat.

Composition The process of setting type.

Concordance The list of primary words, names, etc. that form the foundation of a computerized index.

Condensed A more compact version of typeface.

Content editing The process of evaluating a manuscript for style, organization and large general revisions.

Co-op Where a group of people share the costs of such things as advertising or publishing.

Copy The text of a book.

Copy-editing Technical editing of a manuscript for spelling, grammar, punctuation and consistency.

Copyright The right of a person to retain or sell copies of artistic works that they have produced.

Copyright infringement Unauthorized and illegal use of copyrighted material.

Copyright notice A notice that protects publicly distributed information and must include the symbol and the word "copyright".

Cropping Placing pencil marks at the margins and corners to indicate what portion of a photo or illustration is to be omitted.

Cross reference A reference made from one part of a book to another.

Cutline Another term for caption.

Database A collection of data stored in the computer's memory in such a way that it can be retrieved in a different order.

Dedication Inscription honouring the person or persons who inspired the book. Part of the FRONT MATTER.

Demographics A profile of a group based on such criteria as age, sex, marital status, education, and socioeconomic level.

Desktop publishing Near typeset quality and printed publications done with a computer.

Die cut The creation of openings, shapes or folds by cutting away part of the paper stock.

Direct mail Promotional material mailed directly to potential customers.

Display ad A print advertisement that is larger than a classified ad.

Display type Larger or boldface type for heads, subheads, etc.

Drop cap A large capital letter dropped into text at the beginning of a line; usually used at the beginning of a chapter.

Dummy A rough layout of how the finished book is to appear.

Duotone A process for producing an illustration in two colours from a one colour original.

Dust cover The paper wrapper that goes around the cover of a hardcover but is not stuck on. Also called a *dust jacket*.

Editing Making or suggesting changes in a manuscript.

Edition One or more printings of a work that are basically the same. Can be a revised edition, first edition, or limited edition.

Editor in Chief Top editorial executive in a publishing firm.

E-publishing Publishing a book in a format readable by a computer or specialized reader.

Em Unit of typographical and linear measurement based on the capital letter "M".

En A measurement used in casting off equivalent to half an "M".

Endpapers The leaves of paper at the front and end of a book which cover the inner sides of the boards securing the book to its case.

Engraving The design or lettering etched on a plate or block.

Enlargement Photographic process of creating an image larger than the original.

Epilogue A concluding section that rounds out a story and often updates the reader.

Errata Errors found after the book is printed.

Excerpt A portion taken from a longer work.

Exclusive A news or feature story printed by one source ahead of its competitors.

Extract An excerpt.

Face Short for *typeface*. In computer terms it is called the font.

Facing page Any page forming a double spread with another as seen when the book is open.

Fair use The allowable and legal use of a limited amount of copyrighted material without getting permission.

Film lamination A glossy coating for book covers that protect against scuffing and keeps covers from curling.

First serial rights The right to serialize a printed work prior to publication.

Flap That part of the jacket of a hardcover book that is folded so as to lie between the endpapers and front and back.

Flap copy The text describing the book and the author which appear on the inside flap of hardcover books.

Flat fee A negotiated set fee that an author or illustrator receives for a job of work.

Flier Inexpensive advertising printed on 8 ? X 11 paper.

F.O.B. Free on Board. The quoted price does not include delivery costs.

F and Gs Folded and gathered pages. Sheets that have been folded and collated but not finally trimmed or sewn, sent to the publisher for approval before printing begins.

Folio The page number printed on the text page.

Font Particular cut of a typeface.

Foreign rights Subsidiary rights allowing a work to be published in another country or in other languages.

Foreword Introductory remarks by someone other than the author about the book and its author. Part of the book's FRONT MATTER.

Format The general style or appearance of a book.

Formatting The process of designing a publication.

Freelancer Someone who is self-employed and sells their writing, artistic, editing services on a contract basis to publishers.

Front matter The pages preceding the body of a book. Also called prelims.

Frontispiece An illustration facing the title page. Also called front plate.

Fulfillment Filling and shipping book orders.

Galleys Proofs from the typesetter before the copy has been divided into pages.

Gathering Placing the sections of a book in the correct order for binding.

Genre A category of writing such as science fiction, mystery, romance, etc.

Ghostwriting Writing a book in conjunction with someone else as if it had been written by that other person.

Glossary List giving definitions of terms related to a particular subject. Part of the BACK MATTER.

Glossy A photograph with a shiny finish rather than a matte finish.

Graphics Illustrations other than photographs.

Gutter The inside centre margins of a book.

Gutter bleed An image allowed to extend unbroken across the central margins of a spread.

Half-title A page with the title and publisher's name only printed on it that immediately precedes the title page.

Halftone Process by which continuous tone of photographs is simulated by a pattern of dots of varying sizes.

Hanging indent Form of typesetting in which the initial line of each paragraph is set full measure and the remaining lines are indented.

Hardcover book A cased book with a board cover.

Head The margin at the top of a page.

Heading The title introducing a chapter.

House style The style of spelling, punctuation and spacing used in a printing or publishing house to ensure consistency.

Illustrations Photographs, drawings, graphs and tables used in a book to explain or supplement the text.

Image area Amount of space given to a particular image in design and printing.

Impression All copies of a book printed at the same time from the same type or plates.

Imprint The name of the publisher with place and date of publication.

Imprint page The page carrying the details of printing, copyright, etc. Also called biblio.

In print Books and other publications that are currently available from the publisher.

Index The section of a publication giving alphabetical listing of subject, proper names, etc. mentioned in the book with page references.

ISBN International Standard Book Number.

Justify To space out lines of type so that both margins are aligned.

Kern To adjust the space between selected pairs of characters.

Layout The design for how the printed material, including illustrations, will look.

Leading The space added between lines of type.

Leaf In a book, a single sheet of paper comprised of one page printed on each side.

Libel Written defamation of character.

Ligature Certain letters traditionally joined to form a single character.

Limited edition A limited quantity of books printed.

Line copy or line art Solid black and white copy for reproduction.

List All the titles a publisher has in print and for sale.

List price The retail price of a book before discount.

Lowercase The uncapitalized letters of a typeface.

Manuscript A book before it is typeset and printed. Abbreviated as Mss.

Margin The white space that surrounds the text on a page.

Markup The process of marking a manuscript with directions for the typesetter.

Mass-market paperback The small paperbacks designed for mass market sales.

Master Original camera ready artwork.

Measure The width of a full line of type, usually measured in points and picas.

Model release A form giving permission to use a photo of a person in your publication.

Net receipt Money received by the publisher after discounts.

News release A one page story about the author or book sent to media for promotion.

Notched binding A type of adhesive binding in which the untrimmed spin is notched and roughened before being force fed with glue.

Offset printing The transfer of an inked image to paper using a rubber blanket.

Opaque To paint portions of a negative so it cannot reproduce.

Out of print A book that is no longer available because there are none left in print.

Orphan The first line of a new paragraph that appears by itself at the bottom of a page.

Overrun The extra number of books the printer may produce and should not exceed 10%.

Pagination Numbering, in order, the pages of a book.

Paperback A softcover book with a paper cover.

Paste up The camera ready original prepared for offset printing.

PE Printer's error, used in correcting a proof.

Pen name A pseudonym used to conceal the author's real name.

Perfect binding A squared spine made by gluing the ends together.

Permission Authorization from a copyright holder to quote material.

Pica A typographic measurement equal to 12 points. Six picas equal one inch.

Plagiarism Copying another author's work and taking credit for it as your own.

Plastic binding A type of binding using a plastic spiral or comb.

Plate The printing master containing the image to be printed.

Point A typographic measurement equal to 1/72 inch.

Point of purchase display Book racks, bookmarks, posters, and other sales material given to booksellers to promote the book.

PPI Pages per inch is used to describe thickness of paper stock.

Preface Introductory remarks written by the author. Part of the FRONT MATTER.

Prelims The pages of a book that you have before the actual text or body begins.

Prepack Point of purchase countertop or floor display made of cardboard and filled with your books.

Press kit Publicity materials in presentation folder sent to the media.

Press release Also called a news release.

Press run The number of copies of a book printed at one time. Also called a print run.

Promotional material Any printed matter that promotes the book.

Proof A page of text or photographs that shows what the end product will look like.

Pseudonym A pen name.

Publication date The date when a book is officially considered available for purchase.

Public domain Material that is not protected by copyright.

Quote Exact copy of copyrighted original wording from another source, and enclosed in quotation marks.

Recto The right hand page of a book.

Remainder Leftover books that are sold for a fraction of their cost in order to make space.

Reprint A new printing of a book.

Retouching Touch up a photograph to correct

flaws.

Returns Books that have not been sold are returned to the publisher for a refund or credit.

Review An evaluation of a book made available to the public.

Review copy A complimentary copy of a book sent to a reviewer.

Revised edition A new edition of a book containing substantial new or updated material.

Rights The various rights to publish a work in any form.

Running head Copy set at the tops of printed pages outside the text area informing the reader of the location of the work.

Saddle stitching Binding a book by driving staples through the fold at the centre.

Sans serif A letter or typeface without serifs as in sans serif.

SASE Self-addressed stamped envelope.

Second serial rights The rights for a magazine to run an excerpt after the publication date.

Self cover A cover for a pamphlet, etc. made of the same paper as the text pages.

Serif The short ending stroke of a character in a typeface.

Short run A small print job of less than 500 books best handled by a POD printer.

Shrink wrap Clear plastic wrap used to keep books from being damaged while shipping.

Signature The multiples of pages that books are printed in for offset printing.

Simultaneous editions Releasing both hard cover and soft cover at the same time.

Sinkage The space from the top margin of a text page to the first printed element on the page.

Slipcase A protective box in which a set of books is placed with the spines facing outward.

Small caps Capital letters the same height as lower case letters.

Smythe sewn Signatures are sewn together before the hard cover is glued on.

Spine The back of a book binding.

Spine out When a book is displayed on a shelf so that the spine faces out.

Spiral binding A continuous wire binding threaded through holes punched near the back margin.

Stock Paper used for printing or binding.

Style sheet A guide for editorial or typographic decisions used to ensure consistency.

Subsidiary rights Additional rights that can be sold in addition to the book.

Subsidy publisher A company that charges writers to print their book and puts its own ISBN on the legal page thereby owning the book.

Subtitle An additional title usually used to clarify the actual subject of a non-fiction book.

Table of contents A list in the PRELIM that gives the name of chapters and what page number they start on.

Table of illustrations A list in the PRELIM that notes illustrations and what page they are on.

Tail margin The bottom margin on a page.

Tear sheets Newspaper or magazine reviews, ads or articles cut or torn out.

Terms The number of days before the customer must pay an invoice.

Text The main body of type.

Title Refers to all books the publisher has in print.

Title page The recto page that gives the book's name, author, publisher, and place and date of publication.

Trade paperback A larger paperback.

Trade publisher Commercial publishing house that typically pays authors a royalty to publish and sell their book.

Trim size The dimensions of a full page including the margins, given in inches.

Typeface The style characteristics of a complete font type which usually has a name.

Type styles Type characteristics of a more general kind than those of the various typefaces.

Typographer A type designer or someone who sets type.

Underrun When the printer makes less copies than were ordered.

Unit cost The cost of each book after all expenses have been taken into consideration.

Uppercase The capital letters of a typeface.

Vanity press A subsidy publisher.

Varnish A shiny protective coating applied to a book's cover.

Velo binding A fused plastic binding.

Verso A left hand page.

Web press A printing press that uses roll fed paper rather than sheets.

Wholesaler A company who buys from a publisher and resells to booksellers.

Widow The last line of a paragraph that appears alone at the top of a new page.

Working title The title of a book used while it is being written.

x-height The height of the lowercase letter x in a particular typeface.

BIBLIOGRAPHY

Anderson, Scott, ed. *The Book Trade in Canada: Your complete guide to the Canadian publishing marketplace.* 1998 ed. Toronto: Quill & Quire, 1998

Applebaum, Judith. *How To Get Happily Published.* New York: Harper & Row, Publishers Inc, 1988

Bates, Jem. *The Canadian Writer's Market.* Toronto: McClelland & Stewart Inc, 1996

Brucker, Virgina. *Your Marketing Plan.* Nanoose Bay, BC: We Believe Publications, 2003

The Chicago Manual of Style: The Essential Guide for Writers, Editors, and Publishers. 14th ed. Chicago and London: The University of Chicago Press, 1993

Colombo, John Robert.*The Dictionary of Canadian Quotes.* Toronto: Stoddart Publishing Company Ltd, 1991

Crook, Marion, and Nancy Wise. *How to Self Publish and make money: Writing, publishing and selling your book in Canada*. Kelowna, BC: Sandhill Publishing/Crook Publishing, 1997

Desauer, J.P. *Book publishing: A basic introduction*. New York: Continuum, 1989

Deval, Jacqueline. *Publicize Your Book!: An Insider's Guide to Getting Your Book the Attention It Deserves*. New York: The Berkley Publishing Group, 2003

Garner, Joe. *Never forget the good times: A story of life in British Columbia*. Nanaimo, BC: Cinnibar Press, 1995

Holt, Robert Lawrence. *How to Publish, Promote & Sell Your Own Book*. New York: St. Martin's Press, 1985

Kremer, John. *1001 Ways to Market Books: for authors and publishers. 5th ed*. Fairfield, IA: Open Horizons, 1998

Media Weavers. *Writer's Northwest Handbook. 4th ed*.

Nicholas, Ted. *How to Self-Publish Your Own Book & Sell a Million Copies*. Enterprise-Dearborn, 1993

Poynter, Dan. *The Self-Publishing Manual: How to write, print and sell your own book. 10th ed*. Santa Barbara, CA: Para Publishing, 1997

————. *Writing Nonfiction: Turning Thoughts*

into Books. Santa Barbara, CA: Para Publishing, 2000

Poynter, Dan, and Mindy Bingham. *Is There a Book Inside You?: How to Successfully Author a Book Alone or Through Collaboration*. Santa Barbara, CA: Para Publishing, 1985

Reiss, Fern. *The Publishing Game: Publish a Book in 30 Days!*. Boston: Peanut Butter and Jelly Press, 2003

———. *The Publishing Game: Bestseller in 30 Days!*. Boston: Peanut Butter and Jelly Press, 2003

Rogers, Geoffry. *Editing for Print*. Writer's Digest Books, Cincinnati: 1985

Ross, Tom, and Marilyn Ross. *Marketing Your Books: A collection of profit making ideas for authors and publishers*. Buena Vista, CO: Communication Creativity, 1990

———. *The Complete Guide to Self-Publishing*. 3rd ed. Cincinnati: Writer's Digest Books, Cincinnati: 1994

INDEX

Q

R

W

Did you borrow this book?

If you want to own a copy for yourself, go to www.selfpublishing.ca to order.

Your Writing and Resource Notes